Cambridge Elements ≡

Elements in England in the Early Medieval World
edited by
Megan Cavell
University of Birmingham
Rory Naismith
University of Cambridge
Winfried Rudolf
University of Göttingen
Emily V. Thornbury
Yale University

CRIME AND PUNISHMENT IN ANGLO-SAXON ENGLAND

Andrew Rabin
University of Louisville

T0287056

CAMBRIDGE
UNIVERSITY PRESS

CAMBRIDGE
UNIVERSITY PRESS

University Printing House, Cambridge CB2 8BS, United Kingdom

One Liberty Plaza, 20th Floor, New York, NY 10006, USA

477 Williamstown Road, Port Melbourne, VIC 3207, Australia

314–321, 3rd Floor, Plot 3, Splendor Forum, Jasola District Centre,
New Delhi – 110025, India

79 Anson Road, #06–04/06, Singapore 079906

Cambridge University Press is part of the University of Cambridge.

It furthers the University's mission by disseminating knowledge in the pursuit of
education, learning, and research at the highest international levels of excellence.

www.cambridge.org
Information on this title: www.cambridge.org/9781108932035
DOI: 10.1017/9781108943109

First published 2020

A catalogue record for this publication is available from the British Library.

ISBN 978-1-108-93203-5 Paperback
ISSN 2632-203X (online)
ISSN 2632-2021 (print)

Crime and Punishment in Anglo-Saxon England

Elements in England in the Early Medieval World

DOI: 10.1017/9781108943109
First published online: August 2020

Andrew Rabin
University of Louisville

Author for correspondence: Andrew Rabin, andrew.rabin@louisville.edu

Abstract: Arguably, more legal texts survive from pre-Conquest England than from any other early medieval European community. The corpus includes roughly seventy royal law codes, to which can be added well over a thousand charters, writs, and wills, as well as numerous political tracts, formularies, rituals, and homilies derived from legal sources. These texts offer valuable insight into early English concepts of royal authority and political identity. They reveal both the capacities and limits of the king's regulatory power, and in so doing, provide crucial evidence for the process by which disparate kingdoms gradually merged to become a unified English state. More broadly, pre-Norman legal texts shed light on the various ways in which cultural norms were established, enforced, and, in many cases, challenged. And perhaps most importantly, they provide unparalleled insight into the experiences of Anglo-Saxon England's diverse inhabitants, both those who enforced the law and those subject to it.

Keywords: Law, Old English, Anglo-Saxon, early Middle Ages, English history

ISBNs: 9781108932035 (PB), 9781108943109 (OC)
ISSNs: 2632-203X (online), 2632-2021 (print)

Contents

1 Introduction: Defining Law   1

2 Making Law   6

3 Breaking Law   24

4 Enforcing the Law   43

5 Conclusion: Thinking Law   56

   Bibliography   58

   Acknowledgments   67

1 Introduction: Defining Law

Everything can be called into question in England except the fact that it was conquered in 1066. England is the land of law and of the most scrupulous respect for the law; but the law begins at that date only, or England as such ceases to exist.

- Jean Anouilh, *Becket, or the Honor of God*

"We learnt the dates of the kings and queens of England at school," said Morse. "Trouble is we started at William the First."

"You ought to have gone back earlier, Inspector – much earlier."

- Colin Dexter, *The Jewel that was Ours*

Sometime in the final decade of the tenth century, two wealthy landowners, Wynflæd and Leofwine, fell into dispute over a set of estates near Datchet in Berkshire. The charter recording the dispute tells us that Wynflæd initially presented her claims directly to King Æthelred (r. 978–1016) accompanied by Archbishop Sigeric of Canterbury, Bishop Ordbriht of Selsey, *ealdorman* Ælfric of Winchester, and the king's mother Ælfthryth as witnesses. Æthelred then ordered Archbishop Sigeric to summon Leofwine to court, but he – surprisingly considering the authority of those calling for his presence – refused to appear. Possibly pointing to the laws of King Edgar (r. 959–75) decreeing that royal appeals cannot precede local judgment, Leofwine demanded that the king withhold his ruling and recognize the jurisdiction of the regional shire-court.[1] Forced to yield, Æthelred sent his seal to the court judges along with the commission that they should resolve the dispute in a way "swa rihtlice geseman swa him æfre rihtlicost þuhte" (that ever seemed most just to them). In this second proceeding, Wynflæd produced an even more impressive array of witnesses including more than twenty-five members of the church and nobility, again led by Ælfthryth. Leofwine's witnesses are not recorded, but they too must have been impressive for the case ultimately ended in a compromise. Had it not done so, the judges predicted, "þær syþþan nar freondscype nære" (thereafter there would be no friendship).[2]

---

[1] *III Edgar* 2 and 5–5.2. Old English royal legislation is referred to by the name of the king under whom it was issued. In what follows, when referencing the king's person, his name will be in roman font. When referencing his laws, the king's name will be italicized and, if he has issued multiple law codes, prefaced by a roman numeral. All quotations from Old English royal legislation are taken from Liebermann, *Gesetze*. Accessible translations are available in Attenborough, *Earliest Laws* and Robertson, *Laws of the Kings of England*. Unless otherwise noted, all translations in this Element, both from the laws and other documents, are my own.

[2] S 1454. Charters will be cited by their index number in Sawyer, *Anglo-Saxon Charters*. An updated version of Sawyer's index can be found online at https://esawyer.lib.cam.ac.uk. A selection of charters with accessible translations can be found in Robertson, *Anglo-Saxon Charters*. The text for S 1454 has been taken from Brooks and Kelly, *Charters of Christ Church Canterbury*, no. 133, vol. II, pp. 987–93.

The lawsuit between Wynflæd and Leofwine is striking, not just for what it reveals about early medieval dispute resolution, but also for what it suggests about the character of pre-Conquest legal culture more generally. Historians differ over the efficacy of early law and its role in the governance of the kingdom: some view legal authority during this period as diffuse and largely subject to the customs and practices of local communities, while others see an effective centralized bureaucracy ruled by a powerful and interventionist monarch.[3] Yet neither version of early English legal culture fully reflects the decisions, assumptions, and practices of the participants here. Rather, disagreements regarding jurisdiction, royal prerogative, land tenure and inheritance, judgment and compromise, and even the relative value of justice (*riht*) and friendship (*freondscype*) suggest that the king, court, witnesses, and disputants all approached the process of adjudication with very different perspectives on the law and the authority under which it was administered. The legal world of the dispute is neither entirely local nor fully centralized; instead, it consists of a series of complex negotiations between different centers of authority – the royal court, the church, the regional aristocracy, and the local courts – in which each seeks to assert its own view of law in order to claim precedence over the others. Within this context, Æthelred's command to the judges that the case be decided in the manner that seemed "rihtlicost" (most just) invites the reader to ask whether those involved in the dispute all understood what it meant to be "most just" in the same way.[4] What royal expectations (or demands) did Æthelred's commission imply? What did it mean to command that the dispute be settled according to *riht* as opposed to *laga* (law)? And to what degree were concepts of *riht* shaped by factors such as social class, regional background, gender, and (perhaps most importantly) self-interest? In offering a concise introduction to the legal world of Anglo-Saxon England, this Element will try to suggest at least the beginnings of an answer to these questions.

Any answer, of course, must start with the texts themselves. Arguably, more legal texts survive from pre-Conquest England than from any other early medieval European community.[5] These include approximately seventy acts of legislation along with well over a thousand charters, writs, wills, manumissions and royal diplomas. Also to be included are numerous quasi-legislative texts,

---

[3] A summary of the case for a more centralized government can be found in Campbell, "The Late Anglo-Saxon State," 1–30; Wormald, "God and King," 333–58, especially 48–54., and more recently in Baxter, "The Limits of the Late Anglo-Saxon State," 503–515; and Reynolds, *Deviant Burial Practices*. For counter-arguments, see Hyams, "Feud and the State," 1–43; Rabin, "Capital Punishment," 181–200; Lambert, *Law and Order,* 1–26.

[4] See also Kennedy, "Law and Litigation, 182–183; Rabin, "Law and Justice," 86–91.

[5] For the most influential recent surveys of the laws and legal texts of pre-Conquest England, see Wormald, *Making* and Hudson, *Oxford History.*

legal formularies and rituals, and homilies derived from legal sources. The corpus ranges from the earliest Old English text of any substance, the laws of Æthelberht of Kent (r. c. 589–616), to the latest in the form of post-Conquest land grants. Legal compendia such as the laws of Alfred (r. 871–99) or Cnut (r. 1016–35) suggest a desire to comprehensibly regulate the legal activities of the kingdom and its subjects, while other texts, some as short as a sentence or two, represent limited rulings on specific issues. Some texts refer to the king as *imperator, casere,* or *basileus* – terms evocative of Roman imperial kingship[6] – while others embrace a language of rule grounded in the formulaic structure and phrasing of traditional Old English poetry.[7] Taken together, the laws, charters and similar documents demonstrate the breadth and diversity of pre-Conquest legal thought, yet they also indicate just how porous the boundary between "legal" and "non-legal" texts could be. Æthelred's later laws initially appear to be traditional legislation, but they also frequently lapse into the homiletic cadences of their putative author, Archbishop Wulfstan of York (d. 1023). Likewise, the great legal anthology Cambridge, Corpus Christi College MS 383 (C.C.C.C. 383) contains what looks like a treaty between King Edward the Elder and the Viking King Guthrum, yet the text is an eleventh-century fiction interpolated into the legal record nearly one hundred years after it claims to have been written. Also included in both C.C.C.C. 383 and the other major manuscript source for early English law, the *Textus Roffensis,* is a charm against cattle theft – a genre seldom considered "legal" by modern scholars and omitted from standard editions of pre-Conquest laws but which the anonymous compilers of the manuscripts nonetheless viewed as an appropriate text to accompany royal legislation. Elsewhere one finds passages of legislation that scan like verse, portions of saints' lives that read like charters, and religious rituals that echo royal legislation, among many other examples of cross-genre fertilization. Highlighting such overlaps is not meant to suggest that the Anglo-Saxons saw no distinction between the drafting of laws or charters and other forms of writing. Rather, it is to point out that legal composition frequently incorporated other genres and was incorporated by them in turn. Even though individual laws and charters are only rarely cited with any sort of specificity, the language and rituals of the law permeated the textual world of pre-Conquest England, shaping perceptions of authority and defining the parameters of early English society.

Yet recognizing pre-Conquest legal texts as both hybrid and normative should not detract from our view of Anglo-Saxon law as *law,* that is, as

---

[6] It should be noted, however, that there is only limited evidence for pre-Norman lawmakers' familiarity with Roman law. See Winkler, "Roman Law"; Wormald, *Making,* 96–97; Porter, "Terminology," and section 2.1.

[7] See sections 2.3 and 2.4.

a regulatory instrument designed to ensure the stability and security of community and kingdom. It should, however, make us wary of imposing modern notions of law on premodern legal culture. The laws of pre-Conquest England differ from contemporary Anglo-American legal practice in significant ways, perhaps the most important of which being the absence of distinction between public and civil wrongs (in modern terms, between crime and tort). Likewise, pre-Conquest law also did not distinguish between what would come to be known as felony and misdemeanor.[8] Rather, wrongs to persons or their property were understood, particularly in the earliest texts, as violations against an individual and their family. Accordingly, the responsibility for pursuing redress lay with the kin group rather than a state-sponsored apparatus of legal enforcement. As a result, disputes over land ownership and accusations of theft or other forms of injurious behavior were often treated in similar ways: the accused would not be "arrested" in any modern sense; rather a complaint was brought by the aggrieved party to the shire court. Depending on the status of those involved, a certain number of witnesses – much like those martialed by Wynflæd – would be required of each side in order to testify to the truth or falsehood of the accusation. In certain circumstances, the court might also order the accused to undergo an ordeal to demonstrate innocence or guilt. Once the accusation had been proven to the court's satisfaction, it then assessed an appropriate penalty in the form of a fine, confiscation of property, the loss of a limb, exile, or death. Lawsuit records indicate that appeals were possible, though the frequency of appeals and their chances of success are unknown. That said, accusations were a tricky business in Anglo-Saxon England, and if the ownership of an estate could not be demonstrated unequivocally or its owner could not be fully exonerated of some misdeed, then it was not uncommon for the crown or church to snap up any estates involved for itself.

This brief account summarizes in broad terms how a pre-Conquest legal dispute might proceed, yet as the historian Patrick Wormald cautions, the "'typical' Anglo-Saxon dispute settlement (if there was any such thing) remains elusive."[9] In the absence of official court records, accounts of disputes were largely drawn up by those who benefited from the settlement or their heirs, and only then if they had access to scribes or were literate themselves. Under such circumstances, there can be little surprise that the majority of surviving lawsuits involve the church, and that the majority of those are cases in which the church profited in some way. Yet whether a dispute involved the church or the laity, for

---

[8] O'Brien, "From *Morðor* to *Murdrum*," 321–357; Lambert, "Theft, Homicide and Crime," 3–43; Lambert, "Royal Protections and Private Justice," 157–76; and Kamali, *Felony and the Guilty Mind in Medieval England*, 20–24.

[9] Wormald, "Charters, Law, and the Settlement of Disputes," 292.

the legal historian the same problem remains: those recording a dispute were frequently invested in its resolution, and accordingly concepts of right (*riht*) and law (*laga*) were treated in a manner which reflected the perspective of the account's sponsor. In other words, those responsible for the production of royal legislation, lawsuit narratives, and ecclesiastical records treated the issues at hand – to recall Wynflæd and Leofwine – in a way "that seemed most just to them." The capacity to define *riht*, not just on its own but in a way that superseded other definitions, thereby became a means of claiming and defending legal prerogatives. And for those asserting their *riht* to privileges or property – whether the church, king, or laity – their use of the term was often framed in such a way as to preclude the claims of others. Thus, for Archbishop Wulfstan of York, writing in the early eleventh century, the phrase *Godes riht* encompassed both the dues owed to the church and, more broadly, the divinely ordained legal precedence that was the church's due.[10] In contrast, the laws of Alfred decree that those guilty of breaking bail must be punished as "riht wisie" (the law directs) and *I Æthelstan* (c. 925 × 939) commands the king's reeves to procure for him that which "mid rihte gestrynan magan" (may be rightfully obtained for [him]). Lower on the social scale, an otherwise unknown landowner named Toki was deemed to have "riht . . . gedon" (done right) to pursue a claim to properties that had been bequeathed to him by his wife for his lifetime but which had been prematurely appropriated by the church.[11] These are just three illustrative instances and analogous ones could easily be found depicting similar uses of other words for law such as *dom*, *æw*, and *laga*.[12] My point in highlighting these examples is not simply to observe that the semantic field of *riht* encompasses concepts such as law, justice, fairness, appropriateness, and the rightful claim to both loyalty and tax revenue. Instead, it is to highlight that in any given instance the claim to *rihtness* can be made by multiple parties representing diverse institutions whose views of *riht* may be, not just different, but at odds with one another.

The guiding principle principal of this Element is that pre-Conquest notions of law and justice were not necessarily objective, widely recognized, and with communally agreed upon standards, even if – indeed, especially if – they were often portrayed as such. Rather, claims of *riht*, especially when that *riht* is in dispute, represent moments when the definition of legal authority has become a matter of competition and negotiation. The capacity of an individual or

---

[10] Rabin, *Political Writings*, 36–37.

[11] *Alfred* 3, *I Æthelstan* 5, and S 1474, ed. O'Donovan, *Charters of Sherborne*, no. 17, pp. 59–61.

[12] *Laga* poses a particular problem for the historian as it likely derives from Old Norse and was used initially to refer to legal practices in the Danelaw, in other words, laws that were not seen as "English." See, for instance, *IV Edgar* 2.1.

institution to define, issue, exploit, or circumvent the law served as an indicator of their power and agency within pre-Conquest society. And as the following sections will show, when views of the law came into conflict, determining what was *rihtlicost* could be a very difficult matter indeed.

2 Making Law

Amid the growing turmoil of the early eleventh century, the homilist and legislator Archbishop Wulfstan of York embarked upon an ambitious program of political reform intended to encourage the spiritual and social renewal of the increasingly fragile English kingdom. Wulfstan outlined his program in a series of short, interconnected chapters referred to by modern editors as *The Institutes of Polity*. The model of society set forth in the *Institutes* was grounded in Wulfstan's view that the people of the realm each fell into one of three categories:

> Ælc riht cynestol stent on þrym stapelum, þe fullice ariht stent. An is *oratores;* and oðer is *laboratores;* and ðridde is *bellatores*. *Oratores* sindon gebedmen þe Gode sculan þeowian and dæges and nihtes for ealne þeodscipe þingian georne. *Laboratores* sindon weorcmen þe tilian sculon þæs ðe eall þeodscype big sceall libban. *Bellatores* syndon wigmen þe eard sculon werian wiglice mid wæpnum. On þyssum ðrym stapelum sceall ælc cynestol standan mid rihte on Cristenre þeode. And awacie heora ænig, sona se stol scylfð; and fulberste heora ænig, þonne hrysð se stol nyðer, and þæt wyrð þære þeode eall to unþearfe.

> Each just throne that stands fully as it should rests upon three pillars: first, *those who pray* (*oratores*); second, *those who labor* (*laboratores*); and third, *those who fight* (*bellatores*). *Those who pray* are the clergy, who must serve God and fervently plead for all the people day and night. *Those who labor* are the workers who must toil for that by which the entire community may live. *Those who fight* are the warriors who must protect the land by waging war with weapons. On these three pillars must each throne rightly stand in a Christian polity. If any of them weaken, immediately the throne will tremble; and if any of them fail, then the throne will crumble to pieces.[13]

Wulfstan was by no means the first to reference the three orders trope – it first appeared in the *Old English Boethius* and can also be found in works by his contemporaries Ælfric of Eynsham and Adalbero of Laon – yet he was the first to fully exploit its potential as a model of Christian governance.[14] For Wulfstan, the spiritual revitalization necessary for a kingdom weakened by poor government, Viking raids, and sinful behavior required the restoration of a social order

---

[13] *Institutes of Polity*, ch. 4, ed. Jost, *Polity,* 55–57. Tr. Rabin, *Political Writings*, 106.
[14] See Powell, "Three Orders" and Moilenan, "Social Mobility."

in which king, priest and peasant all fulfilled the roles assigned to them by the divine intelligence. Underlying this claim was Wulfstan's recognition both that the full investment of each order was necessary to the stability of the kingdom and that each order was characterized by specific needs and obligations distinguishing it from the others. The governance of the realm was thus a delicate balancing act, for "if any of [the orders] fail, then the throne will crumble to pieces."

Yet for Wulfstan the three orders trope was not merely a hypothetical social model; rather, the tripartite division of society served as a metaphor for the relationship between a properly ordered state and the laws governing it. The three orders, Wulfstan wrote, must be "staþelige man and strangie and trumme hi georne mid wislicre Godes lare and mid rihtlicre woruldlage; þæt wyrð þam þeodscype to langsuman ræde. And soð is þæt ic secge: ... arære man unlaga ahwar on lande oððe unsida lufige ahwar to swiðe, þæt cymð þære þeode eall to unþearfe" (diligently steadied, strengthened, and reinforced with God's wise teachings and with just worldly law; in that way they will bring lasting guidance to the people. And what I say is true: ... if injustice is exalted anywhere in the land or evil customs anywhere too eagerly embraced, then the people will be brought entirely to ruin).[15] The enactment of just law accordingly plays a central role in ensuring the realm's political stability and moral virtue. This vision of a society predicated on the collaboration between different political communities offers a useful paradigm through which to understand the range and complexity of pre-Conquest legal practice. The distinct yet mutually dependent character of the three orders illustrates, albeit in broad strokes, the similarly balanced – and at times similarly fraught – relationship between the primary categories of early English legal authority: royal law, ecclesiastical *dicta*, and regional custom. Like the three orders, each category of law represents a different component of the Anglo-Saxon body politic – aristocratic, religious, and local – with its own character, expectations, and conception of authority. However, this appearance of difference cannot mask the fact that the various categories of law – like the different social orders – are never entirely distinct from one another: through comparison, contrast, and overlap, each category of law relies upon the others to ensure its effectiveness and define the boundaries of its jurisdiction. Individually, the different forms of law thus convey a partial sense of how the inhabitants of pre-Conquest England understood the social hierarchy and their place within it; when taken together, they reveal the extent to which Anglo-Saxon notions of identity, community, and social order rested upon the interaction of different, and sometimes opposing, political institutions

---

[15] *Institutes of Polity*, ch. 4, ed. Jost, *Polity*, 57. Tr. Rabin, *Political Writings*, 106–107.

that defined both the explicit laws and implicit norms by which early English society was governed.

2.1 Royal Legislation

The earliest written legislation to survive from pre-Conquest England are the laws of King Æthelberht of Kent, which were promulgated in c. 603. Describing these laws just over a century later, the historian Bede wrote that they were composed:

> iuxta exempla Romanorum, cum consilio sapientium constituit; quae conscripta Anglorum sermone hactenus habentur, et obseruantur ab ea. In quibus primitus posuit, qualiter id emendare deberet, qui aliquid rerum uel ecclesiae, uel episcopi, uel reliquorum ordinum furto auferret; uolens scilicet tuitionem eis, quos et quorum doctrinam susceperat, praestare.
>
> according to the examples of the Romans with the counsel of wise men. They are written in English and are still kept and observed by the people. Among these he set down first of all what restitution must be made by anyone who steals anything belonging to the church or the bishop or any other clergy; these laws were designed to give protection to those whose coming and whose teaching he had welcomed.[16]

For Bede, the principal accomplishment of Æthelberht's legislation was to legitimize the privileges of the church in a manner that echoed the Roman traditions of civil and canon law.[17] Yet the phrase "iuxta exempla Romanorum" (according to the examples of the Romans) hints at another purpose also. Æthelberht was the third in a line of kings to exercise dominance over the whole of southern England as well as a relative (by marriage) of the rulers of Merovingian Francia. As such, his decision to issue written laws "according to the examples of the Romans" can be seen as an ambitious attempt to associate himself with the royal lawmakers of old and his realm with the more powerful kingdoms of the continent.[18]

The importance of written law to the aspirations of Æthelberht and his successors in Kent, Mercia, and Wessex is reflected in the size and scope of the Anglo-Saxon legislative corpus. Nonetheless, historians have relatively little evidence for the processes by which laws were settled upon and the procedures involved in the composition of a legal text. Although the promulgation of law codes was frequently associated with assemblies convened by the

---

[16] Bede, *Historia ecclesiastica,* II.5, ed. Colgrave and Mynors, *Bede's Ecclesiastical History,* 150–51.

[17] Wormald points out that, given the limitations of his sources, Bede may be mistaking Romans for Franks. *Making,* 97.

[18] See also Patrick Wormald, "*Iuxta exempla Romanorum*," 15–27.

king and his counsellors, the minutes of these meetings do not survive (if they
ever existed at all). We do not know whether statutes were determined upon
beforehand by the king or his advisors and then announced to the assembly, or
whether the meeting itself served as the occasion on which laws were negotiated
and established.[19] Indeed, with the exception of Wulfstan of York and possibly
Alfred the Great, we know neither the "authors" of the laws – those responsible
for their style, phraseology, and organization – nor the scribes who wrote them
down.

Yet, if much about the circumstances of Anglo-Saxon lawmaking remains
mysterious, the laws themselves do offer a few clues to the process whereby
royal legislation was produced.[20] The earliest surviving prologue to royal
legislation, that attached to the laws of Hlothhere and Eadric (c. 685× 686),
merely relates that the kings "ecton þa æ, þa ðe heora aldoras ær geworhton"
(added to the law that their ancestors made before).[21] More detailed is the
prologue to the laws of Wihtred (r. 630–725), which recounts the meeting of
"eadigra ge[þ]eahtendlic ymcyme" (a consiliary assembly of great men), who
"fundon mid ealra gemedum ðas domas" (devised, with the consent of all, these
decrees). Present at the assembly were "Birhtwald Bretone heahbiscop, 7 se
ærnæmda cyning; eac þan Hrofesceastre bisceop, se ilca Gybmund wæs haten,
andward wæs; 7 cwæð ælc had ciricean ðære mægðe anmodlice mid þy hersu-
man folcy" (Birhtwald, archbishop of Britain, and the aforementioned king;
also in attendance was the bishop of Rochester, which same was named
Gemund; and each order of the church of that people spoke in accordance
with the loyal people).[22] Wihtred's prologue suggests that the composition of
written law in early Kent involved more than merely transcribing royal decree.
Rather, the emphasis here seems to be on lawmaking as a deliberative process in
which the church assumed a leading role, so much so that Archbishop Birhtwald
comes before the king in the list of attendees. Likewise, considerable value
appears to have been placed on unanimous consent, which the short prologue
mentions twice in its final two sentences. That said, we must remember that
legislative prologues were instruments of legal ideology as much as historical
record, and the manner in which they portrayed events was influenced by
contemporary political circumstances. Despite the prominence accorded
Birhtwald, the depiction of law as primarily an expression of royal will in the

---

[19] Roach, *Kingship and Consent,* 104–21.
[20] On the composition of the Kentish laws and their influence on subsequent legislation, see Oliver, *Beginnings.*
[21] *Hlothhere and Eadric* Pr.
[22] *Wihtred* Pr. On the laws of Wihtred, see also Jurasinski, "Royal Law in Wessex and Kent," 25–44 and Oliver, "Royal and Ecclesiastical Law," 25–44.

laws of Æthelberht, Hlothhere, and Eadric suggests that we should not discount Wihtred's role too much. The primacy attributed to the church may simply have been intended to signify the ecclesiastical orientation of the laws themselves.[23] Accordingly, notwithstanding its depiction here, it seems likely that the assembly was understood as more consultative than legislative. Nonetheless, the prologue's depiction of written law as the product of an advisory assembly consisting of king, church, and laity indicates that, whatever the source of the specific statutes may have been, the composition of the legislation likely reflected the collaborative efforts of the "eadigra ymcyme" as much as the spoken will of the monarch.

A greater emphasis on the royal lawgiver appears in early West Saxon legislation, though here again the advice of church and aristocracy seems to have exercised significant influence. The laws of Ine (c. 688 × 694) are composed in the voice of the king (the prologue's first words are "Ic Ine"), yet the royal speaker emphasizes that his decrees resulted from his "smeagende be ðære hælo urra sawla 7 be ðam staþole ures rices" (consulting, for the saving of our souls and the stability of our kingdom) with "Cenredes mines fæder 7 Heddes mines biscepes 7 Eorcenwoldes mines biscepes, mid eallum minum ealdormonnum 7 þæm ieldstan witum minre ðeode 7 eac micelre gesomnunge Godes ðeowa" (my father Cenred, my bishop Hedde, and my bishop Erconwald, and with all the ealdormen and the leading counsellors of my people, and with an assemblage of God's servants).[24] More so than the laws of Wihtred, Ine's legislation characterizes his decrees as a direct expression of the royal will; however, if law is only made when spoken by the king, this speech must reflect the moral and political values appropriate to rulership – spiritual salvation and governmental stability – as well as the counsel of church and aristocracy. The implication of this passage seems to be that the act of lawmaking, or at least the act of producing a formal written law code, involved an extensive deliberative process in which legal authority emanated from the voice of the king, but the validation of this authority demanded the advice and consent of the church and lay aristocracy.

Perhaps the most famous account of royal lawmaking is that found in the prologue to the laws of Alfred. Like the laws of Ine, this passage professes to be the voice of the king, yet here the act of composing law is described in language more redolent of individual authorship than collaborative legislation.[25] Despite the fact that the text refers to the laws having been "eallum minum witum þas

---

[23] Oliver, *Beginnings*, 264–65.

[24] *Ine* Pr. On the use of the royal voice, see Richards, "Anglo-Saxonism," 43 and Rabin, "Witnessing Kingship," 219–36.

[25] Wormald, *Making*, 416–30 and Oliver, "Who Wrote Alfred's Laws?" 231–55.

geeowde" (placed before all my counsellors) and receiving their approval, the passage's emphasis lies on Alfred's role as legal collector, arbiter, and compositor. According to the prologue, "Ic ða Ælfred cyning þas togædere gegaderode ... þe ure foregengan heoldon, ða ðe me licodon" (Now I, King Alfred, have gathered together those of these [laws] ... which our predecessors observed that pleased me). It continues, "þa ðe me ryhtoste ðuhton, ic þa heron gegaderode, 7 þa oðre forlet" (those which seemed to me to be the most righteous, I gathered here, and I rejected the others).[26] This account characterizes the act of making law as a project similar in conception to the Alfredian translation program, in which major Christian texts were collected, revised, and rendered into Old English. As a number of commentators have noted, Alfred's authority lies in his dual role as lawmaker and lawwriter: royal authority here comes to be identified with textual authority.[27] Yet if the depiction of the king as legal author evokes a key component of the Alfredian royal mythos, it is unlikely that the actual process of legal composition transpired in the way it is represented here. Instead, Alfred's laws were almost certainly composed by members of his court, likely with the involvement of the "palace school" he assembled in imitation of Charlemagne. Although the king served as a centralizing figure around whom coalesced a mythology of lawmaking, the laws themselves reflect in both style and substance a process of composition that more resembled the deliberative practices of his predecessors than the *ipse dixit* legislating of later divine-right monarchs. This resemblance emerges in the rhetorical features of earlier legal prologues preserved here: while Alfred's legislation, unlike that of his forebears, is not associated with a particular meeting of a royal council, the king admits to heeding the advice of his counsellors when deciding which laws to omit, and he echoes earlier prologues in emphasizing that the remaining laws "licode eallum" (pleased them [his advisors] all). Accordingly, even though the prologue to Alfred's laws places the king at the center of the lawmaking process, this may reflect more a change in the ideology of kingship than in the practicalities of lawmaking.[28]

The laws of Alfred prove to be something of an outlier in their depiction of the monarch as the "author" of his laws. The legislation of succeeding kings hearkens back to the rhetorical formulae of the seventh-century prologues in emphasizing the conciliar role of church and aristocracy in determining law. *II Edmund* (c. 939 × 946), for instance, attributes its promulgation to the king's

---

[26] *Alfred* Pr. It should be noted that Alfred was hardly the first to characterize lawmaking in this way. Similar claims can also be found in Roman, Byzantine, and Frankish legal texts.

[27] See, for instance, Rabin, "Witnessing Kingship," 228–29; Wormald, *Making* 277–78; and Carella, "Asser's Bible," 195–206.

[28] Roach, *Kingship and Consent*, 87, 104–105.

considering "mid minra witena geðeahte, ge hadedra ge læwedra, ærest, hu ic mæhte Cristendomes mæst aræran" (with the advice of my counsellors, both clerical and lay, above all, how I might best support the Christian faith).[29] Likewise, the prologue to *II–III Edgar* (c. 962 × 963) characterizes itself as "seo gerædnys, þe Eadgar cyng mid his witena geðeahte gerædde, gode to lofe 7 him sylfum to cynescipe 7 eallum his leodscipe to þearfe" (the decree which King Edgar established with the advice of his counsellors for the praise of God and his own royalty, and the benefit of all his people).[30]

It is only with the rise to prominence of Archbishop Wulfstan of York (Bishop of London, 996–1002; Bishop of Worcester, 1002–16; and Archbishop of York, 1002–23) that we begin to get a clearer picture of the procedures involved in composing legislation.[31] As an ecclesiastic and royal counsellor, Wulfstan not only assumed a leading role in the drafting of law codes but he also produced a sufficiently broad corpus of writings to allow scholars to trace the movement of ideas between legislation and other genres of text. In early works, most notably his 1008 address to the royal council (likely delivered at the assembly responsible for the promulgation of *V Æthelred*), as well as such later texts as the *Institutes of Polity,* one can find patterns of ideas and language either borrowed from or recurring in the royal decrees he composed on behalf of Æthelred and Cnut.[32] For instance, phrases from the 1008 homily such as "we sculan iornlic riht up aræran 7 unriht iorne æfre afyllan" (we must diligently promote justice and abolish all injustice) and "we wyllað þæt mann frið 7 freondscipe rihtlice healde for Gode 7 for worulde" (we desire peace and friendship to be kept rightly before God and the world) reappear with slight variations in *V Æthelred* 1.1–2. Likewise, *Polity*'s injunction that a Christian king must "eallum Godes feondum styrnlice wiðstandan" (fiercely resist all God's enemies) can also be found in expanded form in *II Cnut* 7–7.1. Tracing such recurrences across Wulfstan's writings enables us to gather a vague sense of how legislation came to be drafted: although specific injunctions may have been commanded by the king, the drafting of the decrees reflected the input of the royal counsel, especially its ecclesiastical members. In particular, even if articulated in the "voice" of the king, decrees concerning church law and ritual most likely originated with the ecclesiastical hierarchy, especially the archbishops of Canterbury and York and the bishops of London, Winchester and

---

[29] *II Edmund* Pr.   [30] *II–III Edgar* Pr.
[31] On Wulfstan's role as legislator, see Gates, "Cnut's Territorial Kingship,*The Heroic Age*, n.p.; Lawson, "Archbishop Wulfstan and the Homiletic Element," 565–86; Rabin, *The Political Writings*; Richards, "I–II Cnut," 137–56; Wormald, "Holiness of Society," 225–52; Wormald, "Eleventh-Century Statebuilder," 9–27; Wormald, *Making,* 449–65.
[32] Homily LI, ed. Napier, *Wulfstan,* 274–75. Tr. Rabin, *Political Writings,* 128–29.

Worcester.[33] Accordingly, the king's imprimatur lent the law its authority, yet the words were those of his ecclesiastical and lay advisors, and the decrees reflected a royal agenda grounded in social need, political necessity, and religious obligation.

Taken as a whole, if the evidence of Anglo-Saxon legislating procedures remains sparse, we can draw certain tentative conclusions. The act of lawmaking, centered on the king and the law's authority, rested in part on the illusion that the legislative text preserved his spoken decree. Nonetheless, specific injunctions, the wording of the text, and the organization of statutes all derived from a deliberative process involving the king, his advisors, the church, and members of the upper aristocracy. In the earlier Anglo-Saxon kingdoms, these deliberations took place in connection with the meeting of an assembly made up of the leading figures of the realm. With the consolidation of the early kingdoms, the king's jurisdiction expanded and royal power became more centralized. In consequence, the preparation of legislation likely fell under the purview of a more narrowly constituted set of advisors, who then presented the laws at formal meetings of the court, likely coinciding with major church festivals. Old English legislation thus invites the reader to see it as a productive collaboration, reflecting a variety of political agendas and serving a broad range of ideological needs.

2.2 Wills, Charters, and Royal Diplomas

The issuance of royal legislation, meetings of the king's council, and the gatherings of local assemblies were the occasion for the production of a second, often related, form of legal documentation, namely records concerning the conveyance of land, either in the form of exchange, bequest, benefaction, or royal gift.[34] More than a thousand such documents survive, the majority in Latin but a sizeable number in Old English as well. Most texts of this sort are quite short but some run to multiple pages in their modern editions. With such a large body of material, it can be no surprise that conveyances survive in a variety of forms – some as single sheets, some in cartularies, and some even transcribed in the margins of gospel books or other manuscripts unlikely to be lost or discarded. This variety extends to the content and form of the charters as well. Royal diplomas (documents recording the grant of land) tend to be more stylized, typically including an invocation, a preamble, a clause (when relevant) confirming the consent of the king's counsel, a list of sanctions or anathemata for those who might violate the terms of the document, a dating clause, and a list of witnesses. Likewise, wills generally included a preamble identifying the

---

[33] Roach, *Kingship and Consent,* 104–21.   [34] Roach, *Kingship and Consent,* 77–103.

testator and asserting their right to make the bequest, a list of bequests, the name of one or more executors, and a list of witnesses.[35] On the other hand, the use of a formal diplomatic was not necessarily required in all cases and some charters (especially those issued by private citizens) consist solely of a *narratio* describing the nature of the transaction and the circumstances under which it came about. Thus, although one eleventh-century charter begins, "In ures drihtnes naman hælendes Cristes ic Leofinc bisceop mid þafunge 7 leafe Hearðacnutes cynges 7 þæs arwurþan hiredes æt Wigornaceastre ge iunges ge ealdes gebocige sumne dæl lands minan holdan 7 getreowan þegene þam is Ægelric nama" (In the name of our Lord, the savior Christ, I, Bishop Lyfing, with the consent and permission of King Harthacnut and the honorable community at Worcester, both young and old, grant by charter a certain tract of land to my loyal and faithful thegn named Æthelric), another simply opens with "Se fruma wæs ... " (The beginning of it was ...).[36]

Histories of pre-Conquest law often discount land conveyances as subordinate to or less authoritative than legislation issued by the royal court.[37] However, such an approach misconstrues the relationship between land conveyances and formal legislation as well as the former's role in shaping the legal life of the kingdom. Indeed, the history of documentary property conveyance and that of written royal law are nearly coterminous: the earliest authentic royal diplomas date from the reign of King Hlothhere of Kent while several fabricated charters that may be based on authentic sources are attributed to King Æthelberht.[38] It has been argued that charters were first brought to England either by the Roman missionaries dispatched by Pope Gregory I to convert the island – thus ascribing to them the same origin as the practice of producing written law – or by Archbishop Theodore and Abbot Hadrian (both of Canterbury) a generation later.[39] A third possibility, which has yet to be fully explored, is that the practice of recording property transfers in writing actually predates the Roman mission in much the same way that the formal compilation of laws was likely practiced in England before the arrival of Christianity.[40] Whichever is the case, we can say with certainty that the earliest charters were not dispositive themselves, but rather served merely as a means of recording the formal ceremonies at which the

---

[35] Snook, *Chancery*; Tollerton, *Wills*; and Keynes, *Diplomas*, 28–39.

[36] S 1407 and S 1447, both edited in Robertson, *Anglo-Saxon Charters*, nos. 44 and 94, pp. 90–93 and 180–81.

[37] On the problems this approach raises, see Snook, *Chancery*, 1–7.

[38] The charters attributed to Æthelberht are SS 1–5 (though arguments have been made that S 1 may be authentic). Hlothhere's charter is S 8.

[39] Pierre Chaplais, "Augustine," 526–42, and Snook, "Theodore," 257–90.

[40] See, for instance, Snook, "Theodore," 259–61; Brooks, "Æthelberht," 111–12, 129–30.

exchange of land actually took place (at times through the symbolic exchange of clods of earth from the properties involved).

In many ways, the impression of legal authority conjured by royal legislation can be found in conveyances as well: exchanges of land or other forms of property between the king, the church, and those subjects wealthy enough to own substantial estates. They point to a shared sense of how property ought to be allotted; the representation of Wulfstan's three estates on the witness lists appended to such documents contributes to an image of a well-ordered society; and consistencies of format and language suggest a widespread sense of the forms and formulae needed to make a legal document "official." The similarity of so many charters has even been taken as evidence for the existence of a royal chancery or similar office.[41] Yet while this image of ordered governance is true for a majority of conveyances, closer inspection reveals the presence of a more complicated political world also. In these documents, we come as close as possible to hearing the voices of those such as women or slaves who exist only at the margins of a legal system defined by the king's laws. Likewise, in that such documents were frequently produced for use in or as the result of legal disputes, texts such as wills, charters, and royal diplomas can shed light on what happens when the orderliness of society breaks down. For all their value as historical sources, however, land conveyance documents also have significant limitations. On one hand, they are invaluable for the study of place names, prosopography, and land tenure. Likewise, they present a vivid picture of royal and ecclesiastical authority in action and, in their witness lists, a sense of the rise and fall of political factions, the existence of which might not have been recorded in other sources. At the same time, though, it must be remembered that the perspective of these documents can hardly be called impartial. The majority of conveyances survive because they either benefited a particular religious foundation or had been deposited there by a layperson, and so were preserved in monastic or cathedral archives.[42] Without a similar mechanism for preservation, those charters that do not involve church properties or that cast the church in a bad light have largely been lost. Moreover, for the nobility and church, the production of official documents served as a means of promoting their authority, a function amply served by the texts' elaborate preambles. At a more basic level, conveyances as written documents presume a degree of literacy present in only a small fraction of the population. Particularly open to question are those charters produced at the conclusion of a legal dispute. Texts of this sort were written at the behest of the victorious claimant in order both to

---

[41] Snook, *Chancery*; Keynes, "Royal Government," 226–57; Keynes, *Diplomas*, 14–19.
[42] Wormald, "Handlist," 276–77.

provide a permanent record of the victory and to denigrate as much as possible both the evidence and character of their opponent. This explicit bias speaks to the charter's primary function: whether grant, bequest, or dispute record, the purpose of a charter was to shape the memory of persons and events in order to enable or prevent future actions. In other words, as one historian has put it, each charter "reflects a conscious or unconscious effort to select and organize information from the past for the needs of the present, each reflects an effort to select and organize information from the present for the possible needs of the future."[43] As such, the aim of a simple land grant or bequest is to reclassify property considered *folcland* (land owned without written proof) as *bocland* (land held by right of official record) and thus ensure that the new owner possessed incontrovertible evidence should his rights to the land ever be threatened. In the more perilous circumstances of a legal dispute, the charter served as a kind of preventive law intended to stave off any future action of challenges by the losing claimant or his family.[44] Given this context, it can be no surprise that the records of pre-Conquest legal disputes are filled with instances of charters being strategically misplaced, found, forged, stolen, or destroyed. For example, an early ninth-century property dispute between the archbishop of Canterbury and the Abbey of Minster-in-Thanet ended with the archbishop (the victor in the suit) demanding that all earlier records of the land be destroyed so as to prevent any possibility of challenging his possession.[45] As the archbishop recognized, it was not enough for a victorious litigant to have won control over the disputed property; one must have control over its history as well.

The vast majority of conveyances record relatively straightforward transactions yet two brief examples – both from the reign of Æthelred – illustrate how these texts can reveal the complexities of the pre-Conquest legal world. The first example involves the politics of the royal court. Ascending to the throne in 978 after the assassination of his stepbrother, Æthelred spent much of his early reign antagonizing the church by seizing lands and revoking privileges originally granted by his father, Edgar. Beginning in 993, however, Æthelred did an abrupt about face, issuing a series of five charters that restored to the church much of what had been taken. Collectively referred to as the "penitential charters," the texts are characterized by Æthelred's explicit repentance for the sins of his youth.[46] Thus, a charter issued in 998 includes a passage in which Æthelred is made to say,

---

[43] Brown, "Charters as Weapons" 230. See also Foot, "Reading Anglo-Saxon Charters: Memory, Record, or Story?" 39–67.
[44] Hyams, "The Charter as a Source for the Early Common Law," 173–76.
[45] S 1436. On this dispute see Rabin, "Courtly Habits," 302–303.
[46] Levi Roach, "Penitential Discourse," 258–76; Cubitt, "The Politics of Remorse, 179–92.

Nunc autem quia superna michi parcente clementia ad intelligibilem etatem perueni. et que pueriliter gessi in melius emendare decreui. Idcirco Domini compunctus gratia quicquid tunc instigante maligno contra sanctum dei apostolum me inique egisse recogito. totum nunc coram deo cum flebili cordis contritione peniteo. et queque opportuna ad eundem locum pertinentia libenter restauro.

However, now that I have reached maturity thanks to merciful divine grace, I have decided to make amends for my childhood deeds. Therefore, moved by the Lord's grace, I am reviewing all that I have wrongfully done, driven then by malignant instigation against the holy apostle of God; now, entirely before God, with my heart's tearful remorse, I repent and restore freely that which properly belongs to this place.[47]

Æthelred's change of heart is surprising, and all the more so in that it is expressed in language more redolent of a handbook of penance than a royal diploma. The precise cause of Æthelred's reversal is unknown, yet the witness lists to the penitential charters offer a clue. Among the other distinctive features of these charters is the gradual appearance in their witness lists of a block of bishops, frequently grouped together in more or less the same order. Each of the bishops oversees a diocese associated with the monastic reform movement during the reign of Edgar and, perhaps more importantly, each is associated with Archbishop Ælfric of Canterbury (d. 1005). Accordingly, what the witness lists seem to indicate is the emergence of an increasingly influential faction at court made up of reform-minded bishops and led by Archbishop Ælfric.[48] The evidence of the witness lists thus offers a plausible explanation for Æthelred's change of policy in the early 990s.

The second example is a writ issued in the early eleventh century by Ælfthryth, widow to King Edgar, Æthelred's mother, and among the most powerful members of the royal court.[49] While married to Edgar, Ælfthryth was one of the earliest royal consorts to be formally crowned queen, a title that secured her place at court as more than merely the king's companion in the bedchamber. Her influence was such that Bishop Æthelwold of Winchester (d. 984) wrote in the *Regularis concordia* (973) that it was her special role to "sanctimonialam mandras ut impauidi more custodis defenderet cautissime"

---

[47] S 893, ed. Campbell, *Charters of Rochester*, no. 32, pp. 42–44.

[48] Rabin, "Wulfstan at London," 193–95. On the usefulness of charters to discern political factions, see Keynes, *Diplomas*, 131–56. On the connections between these bishops, see Keynes, "Wulfsige, Monk of Glastonbury," 60; Simon Keynes, "Church Councils, Royal Assemblies," 106; Ann Williams, *Æthelred the Unready*, 37.

[49] Sawyer 1242, ed. Harmer, *Writs*, no. 108, pp. 396–97. On this dispute, see Rabin, "Female Advocacy," 261–88. On the role of charters in pre-Conquest litigation more generally (and with special reference to the dispute between Wynflæd and Leofwine), see Keynes, "Cuckhamsley," 193–210.

(defend communities of holy women as a fearless guardian).[50] Following Edgar's sudden death, Ælfthryth led the court faction seeking to put Æthelred on the throne, an effort that finally came to fruition in 978. The writ in question was issued approximately twenty years later and describes her participation in a dispute involving her kinswoman Wulfgyth. The mere fact that the events described in the text are recounted in a woman's voice and from a woman's perspective make this a remarkable document, yet other features stand out as well. Perhaps most striking is the range of legal functions she fulfilled over the course of the dispute: she acted as an advocate on her kinswoman's behalf; along with Æthelwold, she negotiated the final settlement, and she held the titles to the land to ensure that the terms of settlement were followed. Yet the writ illustrates the limitations on her actions as well. Ælfthryth issued the writ, not as part of the dispute itself, but to serve as (presumably successful) evidence against accusations that she had improperly pressured the litigants into a compromise under which she was the greatest beneficiary. The writ thus illustrates the ways in which female litigants sought the support of female patrons; the types of legal outcomes available to women during this period; how a woman, especially a noble one, might defend herself against charges of illegal behavior; and the strategies through which a woman at court might leverage her influence in a legal context (it should be remembered that she did much the same thing on Wynflæd's behalf in the dispute discussed in the Introduction). In doing so, the record of what initially appears to be a fairly straightforward lawsuit provides valuable insight into one way in which women pursued their interests in a legal context.

Yet despite the writ's value as one of the relatively few surviving examples of women's involvement in legal disputes, it must be remembered that Ælfthryth's position – like that of her predecessors – was an unusually privileged one. Both her status as queen and her specially appointed role as the legal guardian of female monastic communities afforded Ælfthryth a degree of flexibility unavailable even to other aristocratic women. The act of legislating remained the sole preserve of male lawmakers and the imagined readers of the laws were the king's male subjects. Yet even within these limitations, some women did find ways to dictate patterns of land tenure – albeit only in a personal or familial context – and ensure that their intents were recognized. One example can be found in a late tenth-century sequence of wills produced by the *ealdorman* Ælfgar of Essex and his daughters Æthelflæd and Ælfflæd. Ælfgar's will dictated the bequest of family estates to certain religious foundations should his daughters die childless, as indeed they did. In their wills,

---

[50] Symons, *Regularis Concordia*, 2.

however, his daughters incorporate family land into estates they had acquired through purchase or marriage and, although they bequeathed the property to the foundations named by Ælfgar, they did so in their own names rather than that of their father.[51] In effect, the wills of Ælfgar and his daughters depict Æthelflæd and Ælfflæd emphasizing their own agency as legal actors and claiming for themselves the spiritual benefit the bequests conveyed. Though this too was a high-status family, the wills of Æthelflæd and Ælfflæd provide an illustration of women utilizing existing practices of land tenure to govern the disposition of their property and acquire the associated benefits for themselves.

As these examples indicate, much more is to be gained from land conveyances than merely a record of property ownership. Texts of this sort offer a unique perspective on the lived experience of law for the inhabitants of pre-Conquest England. Varied in purpose, style, and composition, they provide vivid evidence for the ways in which Wulfstan's three orders interacted, often productively but at times antagonistically as well.

2.3 Ecclesiastical Law

The church's influence extended into every aspect of pre-Conquest culture, and this was particularly the case when it came to the making of law. Despite the modern tendency to differentiate between the secular and the religious, it is impossible to understand early English legal culture without taking into account the central role played by ecclesiastical law in the governance of the kingdom. So important was the church's role that its imprint can be found on the very first clause of the earliest English written code of law:

> Godes feoh 7 ciricean XII gylde. Biscopes feoh XI gylde. Preostes feoh IX gylde. Diacones feoh VI gylde. Cleroces feoh III gylde. Ciricfriþ II gylde. Mæthl friþ II gylde.

> The property of God and the church shall be compensated with twelve-fold compensation. A bishop shall be compensated with eleven-fold compensation. A priest shall be compensated with nine-fold compensation. A deacon shall be compensated with six-fold compensation. A clerk shall be compensated with three-fold compensation. Violation of the church's peace shall be compensated with two-fold compensation. Violation of an assembly shall be compensated with two-fold compensation.[52]

---

[51] The wills of Ælfgar, Æthelflæd, and Ælfflæd are indexed as S 1483, S 1494, and S 1486 respectively. They are edited in Whitelock, *Anglo-Saxon Wills*, nos. 2, 14, and 15, pp. 6–9, 34–41. On these texts, see Crick, "Women, Posthumous Benefaction, 402–403; Thompson, "Women, Power, and Protection, 13–16.

[52] *Æthelberht* 1. See Oliver, *Beginnings*, 83–84.

Although almost certainly a late addition, this passage nonetheless reflects the powerful influence the church exercised over the composition of royal legislation.[53] We have already seen the importance accorded ecclesiastical authority in the preface to the Kentish laws of Wihtred, an emphasis found in West Saxon law as well: in the legislation issued by Alfred, for instance, the laws of the king were prefaced by passages from Exodus and excerpts from apostolic law. In the mid-tenth century, the legislation of Edgar issued at Andover was split between ecclesiastical (*II Edgar*) and secular laws (*III Edgar*), a pattern that would recur approximately fifty years later in the laws of Cnut (*I–II Cnut*). Equally significant was Edgar's decree that bishops were to sit on regional hundred courts, thereby ensuring their judicial authority over all lawsuits rather than just those involving the church.[54] Perhaps the most elaborate illustration of the church's legal influence, though, can be found in *VII Æthelred* (1009), in which the king commanded that the whole kingdom was to carry out an elaborate series of penitential rituals prescribed by the church in response to the increasingly frequent Viking invasions.[55] At least in theory, then, crown and church were viewed as working in tandem, each reinforcing the authority of the other. This partnership was conceived by Bishop Æthelwold as the result of a contract between God and king. As he writes in the preface to his Old English translation of the Benedictine Rule, "Nu þu mine naman and andweald – þæt is, mine cyricean þe ic rihtlice on minum synderlicum andwealde hæbbe – georne friþast 7 fyrþrast, ic þe to leanes þinne noman mærsige 7 þin rice þe þu under minum andwealde hyltst geeacnige 7 mid gode fyrþrige" (because you [the king] zealously protect and advance my name and dominion – that is, my Church, which I rightly have in my special dominion – as a recompense to you I will glorify your name and increase and advance in prosperity your kingdom which you hold under my dominion).[56]

It would be a too great a task to summarize the myriad ways Æthelwold's vision was reflected in practice, though some general statements can be made regarding the context in which it did so. First, the legal involvement of the English church should not be viewed in isolation from current trends either on the continent or elsewhere in Britain. The guidance that Pope Gregory I offered to the missionaries tasked with converting the English later came to be echoed in the laws of Wihtred; Alfred's laws were shaped by the international cadre of

---

[53] This is a topic taken up most recently and most authoritatively in Jurasinski, *The Old English Penitentials*. Also valuable is the earlier discussion of this issue in Hough, "Penitential Literature and Secular Law," 133–41.

[54] *III Edgar* 5.2.   [55] Keynes, "An Abbot, an Archbishop, and the Viking Raids," 151–220.

[56] Edited and translated as "King Edgar's Establishment of the Monasteries" in Whitelock, *Councils and Synods,* 147.

ecclesiastics he invited to his court in imitation of Charlemagne's "palace school"; and the legislation composed by Archbishop Wulfstan drew from both continental theologians such as Hincmar of Rheims and insular sources such as the *Collectio canonum Hibernensis*. In short, the participation of the pre-Conquest church in matters of what otherwise would be "secular law" should not be seen as an outlier (though it is sometimes treated as such by modern historians), but rather as an expression of what many at the time believed to be one of its essential functions.

Second, the nature of the church's influence reflected a wider variety of ecclesiastical texts than simply those (such as papal bulls or decretals) that might be thought of as obviously legal. The church, like the king and the aristocracy, sought to use legal texts and practices to advance its institutional agenda. Doing so required it to participate in the same sort of negotiation for political power and legal influence that we have already witnessed in both the making of royal law and the conveyance of land. Genres such as handbooks of penance, homilies, and poetry all played a role in shaping English legal culture to fit church orthodoxy. The most obvious examples of this can be found in the works of Archbishop Wulfstan, whose homilies often seem indistinguishable from his legal writings, yet there are many other examples of textual cross-pollination also. Many clauses in the laws of Alfred closely echo passages from pre-Conquest penitentials, and similar echoes can also be found in the laws of his successors Æthelstan, Edmund, Edgar, and Æthelred.[57] These few examples highlight the fact that the church's influence on pre-Conquest legal culture was not merely a matter of explicit interventions at individual assemblies or synods; rather, it reflected one aspect only of the church's permeation of pre-Conquest culture as a whole.

2.4 Custom, Tradition, and Oral Law

It is unfortunate that the laws of local communities and the practices by which they governed themselves should have left only the smallest traces in the textual record. Although written legislation, charters, and ecclesiastical law offer a relatively clear picture of legal authority at the higher echelons of society, it is difficult to tell what part they played in the lives of those lower down the social scale.[58] In an age of limited literacy, it could be difficult for a community – particularly one located far from major cities, religious founda-tions, or the royal court – to fully participate in a legal culture based on the production of written documents. In such communities, oral law and unwritten

---

[57] Jurasinski, *The Old English Penitentials,* 52–85; Marafioti, "Crime and Sin," 60–66.
[58] See Lambert, *Law and Order,* 238–93.

tradition existed alongside the more prestigious written laws of God and king. In part, this reflects that fact that early Anglo-Saxon law generally was composed and transmitted orally, of which echoes survive in the more idiosyncratic clauses of the early Kentish and West Saxon laws. The laws of Ine, for instance, decree

> [43] Ðonne on beam on wuda forbærne 7 yppe on þone ðe hit dyde, gielde he fulwite: geselle LX scill, forþamþe fyr bið þeof.
> [43.1] Gif mon afelle on wuda wel monega treowa 7 wyrð eft undierne, forgielda III treowu ælc mid XXX scill ne ðearf he hiora ma geldan, være hiora swa fela swa hiora være; forþone sio æsc bið melda nalles ðeof.

> [43] If someone sets fire to a tree in a forest, and it becomes known who did it, he is to pay the full penalty: he must pay forty shillings for fire is a thief.
> [43.1] If someone fells a great many trees in a forest and it then comes to be known, he is to pay thirty shillings for each of three trees, nor must he pay more, however many there may be, for an axe is an informer not a thief.[59]

This clause has been the cause of some puzzlement among legal historians. The reason for fire's personification as a thief is clear enough, yet the characterization of an axe is more ambiguous. Many different solutions have been posed – some more ingenious than plausible – but the most likely is that it hearkens back to an earlier oral legal formula, clear enough to the passage's contemporaries but gradually forgotten as law came to be transmitted in writing rather than preserved in memory. A similar memorial function might be at the root of the metrical preface to the early Kentish laws of Hlothhere and Eadric, which, when separated into clauses, display many of the same metrical and alliterative features found in Old English poetry:

Hloþhære 7 Eadric,	Hlothhere and Eadric,
Cantware cyningas,	kings of the men of Kent,
ecton þa æ	extended the laws
þa ðe heora aldoras	that their elders
ær geworhton	previously made
ðyssum domum	with these rulings
þe hyr efter sægeþ.	that are stated hereafter.[60]

Not only does this preface define law as something that is to be *said*, but the use of meter and alliteration – both common features of Old English verse – reflect the practice of oral-formulaic composition common to pre- or marginally

---

[59] On these clauses, see Bremmer, Jr., "Proverbs in the Anglo-Saxon Laws," 174–76.
[60] See also Liebermann, *Gesetze*, III.18.

literate societies. This is not to suggest that the laws of Hlothhere and Eadric were originally composed orally, though that may have been the case; rather, it is to highlight the survival of oral legal practices in the age of written legislation.

Yet if early legislation preserves some trace of what pre-literate law may have looked like, for the most part, we have no way of knowing what the various forms of oral tradition may have looked like in individual communities. This survival of such traditions in an age of literacy may be what stands behind the vague references to *folcriht* (the law of the people) in the legislation of Edmund and Edgar.[61] A slightly more solid example can be found in the dispute between Wynflæd and Leofwine: in settling the suit, the judges dispensed with the formal ceremony of oathtaking because "þær syþþan nar freondscype nære" (thereafter there would be no friendship). The priority was not to determine which claimant had the better legal case, but rather to find a compromise that would preserve the peace of the community. In a situation of this sort, a judgment that conformed to communal needs and practices superseded the obligation to abide by the strict letter of the law. Indeed, it may be that Æthelred's command that the judges do what seemed to them "most just" (*rihtlicost*) represented an implicit acknowledgement that local practice did not always fully conform to the laws of the king.

Moreover, difficult as it may have been to reconcile royal legislation with local practice generally, the relationship between the two was even more complex in places such as the Danelaw or along the borders of Wales and Scotland – places, that is, where cultural differences resulted in different understandings of the law's authority and limits.[62] Evidence for the negotiations resulting from such instances survives in the form of an early eleventh-century treaty (typically referred to, albeit inaccurately, as the *Dunsæte* Ordinance) between the English and Welsh communities on the River Wye somewhat south of modern-day Archenfield. The location is an isolated one, appearing in neither the Burghal Hidage nor *Domesday Book*. The treaty is valuable for two reasons: first, it is the only surviving pre-Conquest legal document produced to address the needs of so small and remote a community; and second, it is one of the few extant legal records that illustrates with such detail how local populations dealt with cultural difference in matters of law. Not surprisingly, its contents – tracing lost or stolen cattle, assaults perpetrated by one community on the other, how to treat guests from across the river, and procedures for the resolution of disputes – all concern the practical challenges involved in keeping the peace between two often fractious populations. What is striking, though, is the extent to which the text draws on both Welsh and English practices to create

---

[61] See *II Edmund* 7 and *I Edgar* 7.   [62] On this point, see Brady, *Borderlands*

something of a legal portmanteau. The nature of this amalgam can be seen in clause 3.2: "xii lahmen scylon riht tæcean Wealan and Ænglan, vi Engliscne and vi Wylisce" (twelve lawmen, six Englishmen and six Welshmen, shall declare what is just to both Welshmen and Englishmen).[63] This clause – which warrants much more discussion than can be given here – applies concepts common to English law (particularly the obligation of a court to "taecen riht" "pronounce justice"[64]) to practices drawn from Welsh tradition (such as the selection of committees of six representatives from different communities to meet and discuss matters of legal controversy).[65] In short, the clause appears to be the result of careful negotiation: the formulation reflects Anglo-Saxon law but the procedures more closely resemble Welsh law. The clause is thus structured in such a way as to permit twelve individuals from two different legal communities to work in concert to resolve potentially explosive disputes. Even though the English and Welsh panelists may reach the same resolution, each can view that resolution as reflecting their own legal traditions and their own conception of justice.

Wulfstan's *oratores*, *bellatores*, and *laboratories* thus inhabited a world governed not by one law, but many: religious and secular, royal and local, written and unwritten. Their interactions with these laws became a way of defining their own identities and that of their communities. Much like the three orders, social coherence and stability depended upon the interaction of the various forms of law and those who made and adhered to them; however, different views of authority, competing interests, and opposing agendas entailed compromises, negotiation, and at times conflict. Perhaps most importantly, the reconciliation of different legal systems provided a means of establishing the rules of permissible behavior and the punishments for those who broke them. For as we shall see, the causes and categories of criminal behavior were very much on the mind of both the makers of law and their subjects – and just as the definition of law became a source of discussion and debate, so too did the definition of lawlessness.

3 Breaking Law

A well-known charter of the late tenth century records King Edgar's approval of a property exchange between Bishop Athelwold of Winchester and one Wulfstan Uccea. The charter's first half documents a complicated series of transactions involving estates at Washington, Yaxley, and Ailsworth, the latter of which was granted by the bishop to Peterborough Cathedral. Although the

---

[63] *Dunsæte* 3.2.   [64] See *I Edgar* 7, *III Edgar* 5.2, and *II Cnut* 18.1.
[65] See, for instance, Jenkins, *Hywel Dda*, 4.

exchange initially appears uncontroversial, the charter's second half records the troubling circumstances under which Wulfstan acquired the estates at Ailsworth:

> [Þ]æt land æt Ægeleswyrðe headde an wyduwe 7 hire sune ær forwyrt forþanþe hi drifon [i]serne stacan on Ælsie, Wulfstanes feder, 7 þæt werð æreafe, 7 man teh þæt morð forð of hire inclifan. Þa nam man þæt wif 7 adrencte hi æt Lundene brigce, 7 hire sune ætberst 7 werð utlah. 7 þæt land eode þam kynge to handa 7 se kyng hit forgeaf þa Ælfsige 7 Wulstan Uccea, his sunu, hit sealde eft Adeluuolde bisceope swa swa hit her bufan sægð

> The land at Ailsworth had previously been confiscated from a widow and her son because they drove an iron nail into Ælfsige, Wulfstan's father, and it was discovered, and that image [*morð*] was taken from her room. Then the woman was taken out and they drowned her at London Bridge, but her son escaped and became an outlaw. The land then went to the king, who gave it to Ælfsige, and his son Wulfstan later gave it to Bishop Æthelwold, just as is narrated above.[66]

This narrative raises more questions than it answers. The text clearly wishes us to view the nameless widow and her son as sinister outcasts practicing forbidden arts on the margins of society. (Grendel too lived only with his mother.) Even the term for the widow's room – *incleofa*, used elsewhere to denote a lion's den – evokes their outsider status. Yet there are a number of details in the text that resist this reading. The property involved was not insignificant – it even warrants mention as a Peterborough holding in the *Domesday Book* more than a century later[67] – suggesting that the widow likely was more well off than the charter seems to suggest. Also curious is the absence of any mention of a trial, a significant omission as drowning (or execution generally) is not otherwise attested as a punishment for witchcraft.[68] The very length of the witchcraft narrative in comparison to the details offered concerning the other properties suggests that the sponsors of the charter were more interested in justifying their ownership of this particular estate than any of the others mentioned in the conveyance. Taken together, such details invite the suspicion that the property was obtained in a questionable fashion and that the purpose of the charter was to legitimize its acquisition by condemning the widow and erasing both her name and that of her heir from the written record.

The witchcraft charter illustrates many of the difficulties involved in the study of legal wrongdoing in Anglo-Saxon culture. The modern distinction between felony and misdemeanor had not yet emerged, nor had distinctions

---

[66] S 1377, ed. Kelly, *Charters of Peterborough*, no. 17, pp. 275–79.
[67] See Williams and Martin, *Domesday Book,* 596.
[68] Davies, "Witches," 50 and Rabin, "Law and Justice," 43–44.

between crime (a legal violation punishable by the state) and tort (a civil wrong against an individual). As a result, the responsibility to seek legal recourse lay with the injured party, in this case Wulfstan Uccea's father. Records in such cases were typically produced by the victorious party without any expectation of objectivity, in this case much to the detriment of the widow and her son. Moreover, those records that do survive constitute only the tiniest fraction of legal documents issued before 1066. Even greater are the number of legal violations that went unrecorded, either because documentation was judged unnecessary or because the parties lacked the wherewithal to produce any. Furthermore, for kings such as Edgar, disputes over property ownership, particularly when criminal activity was alleged, became an opportunity to seize the estates in question in order to redistribute them to their supporters. Perhaps most puzzling, though, is the frequency with which the resolution of disputes and the punishments for lawbreaking appear to differ from the rulings set forth in royal legislation. Indeed, nowhere in the extant records of legal disputes does a plaintiff, defendant, witness, or judge refer to the king's decrees.[69] This is not to suggest that royal law was unread, neglected, or deemed irrelevant to the preservation of public peace. Rather, it provides yet more evidence of the complex legal world of pre-Norman England and the extent to which formal legislation coexisted with both regional custom and practical necessity. Accordingly, in order to understand how the king and his subjects responded to legal wrongdoing, we must answer two questions: what constituted an offence? And who were the offenders?

3.1 What Constituted an Offense?

The many different varieties of wrongdoing in early English legal texts can usefully be divided into three categories: offenses against property, offenses against persons, and offenses against authority.[70]

3.1.1 Offenses Against Property

Historians have long recognized the predominant place held by theft and other forms of property seizure in early English legal thought, a predominance echoed even in such non-legal texts as *Beowulf*, in which an act of theft awakens a dragon. Even as early as the laws of Æthelbert one can find strictures against theft from the church, theft from the king, theft by a freeman from someone of

---

[69] Wormald, "*Lex Scripta* and *Verbum Regis*," 18–9. Wormald later moderated this view, noting that disputes often seem to follow the procedures set forth in royal legislation even if the specific statutes are not cited. See Wormald, "God and King," 348–49; Cubitt, "Lawbook," 1031–33.

[70] For a different categorization, see Hudson, *Oxford History*, 164–68.

the same status, highway robbery using borrowed weapons, theft from an enclosed field or homestead, theft from a slave, and theft by slaves.[71] The value of theft as a category of offense is reinforced by the fact that theft-clauses from *Wihtred* appear nearly verbatim in the contemporary West Saxon laws of Ine.[72] *Wihtred* and *Ine* further decree that a thief caught in the act may be executed without trial.[73] *Wihtred* also awards what can only be described as a bounty to someone who catches a thief later sentenced to death.[74] By the issuance of Æthelstan's "Andover Code" (*II Æthelstan*) nearly 250 years later, it was considered lawful to execute children as young as twelve for stealing anything over the value of eight shillings, though the age was later raised to fifteen.[75] It appears that the aggressive prosecution of thieves may have raised some concern, though: *V Æthelred* 3 decrees that "Cristene men for ealles to litlum to deaðe ne fordeme; ac ells geræde man friðlice steora folce to þearfe, 7 ne forspille for litlum Godes handgeweorc 7 hie agene ceap þe he deore gebohte" (Christians are not to be sentenced to death for too trivial offenses, but instead merciful penalties shall be established for the good of the people, so that the handiwork of God for which he paid dearly be not destroyed for trivial offenses). Despite a certain squeamishness over the use of capital punishment, however, *II Cnut* 26 nonetheless decrees that a convicted thief "hi ne næfre feorh ne gesecan" (will never be able to save his life).[76]

No less important than the theft of movables was the abuse or misappropriation of an owner's rights over landed property. As discussed in the previous section, land tenure could take two forms: *folcland*, according to which land was held by tradition of common consent, and *bocland*, the holding of land by deed, grant, or bequest. The theft or forging of charters was thus a common means of appropriating the property of one's neighbors. The dubious acquisition of land seems to have been a particular problem along the Welsh border, as *V Æthelred* complains of "ætfengan þe swicigende manswican lufedan be westan" (the property seizures, loved by the lying swindlers in the west).[77] A more serious form of property theft was *hamsocn*, a violent raid intended to pillage or seize another's homestead. *II Edmund* rules that those guilty of *hamsocn* must forfeit all their possessions, while *IV Æthelred* forbids the perpetrators from burial in hallowed ground.[78] The seriousness of *hamsocn* is reflected in a tenth-century charter from Hyde Abbey. The charter records that a landowner by the name of Wulfbold plundered his stepmother's estate in order to seize property she had inherited from his father. When he refused to return the stolen goods, the king first confiscated his lands and, when he persisted, later sentenced him to death.

---

[71] *Æthelberht* 1, 4, 9, 19, 28, 89, and 90.   [72] *Wihtred* 28 and *Ine* 20 and 21.
[73] *Wihtred* 26 and *Ine* 12.   [74] *Wihtred* 26.1.   [75] *II Æthelstan* 1.   [76] *II Cnut* 26.1.
[77] *V Æthelred* 32.1.   [78] *II Edmund* 6 and *IV Æthelred* 4.

Wulfbold's violent proclivities seem to have passed on to his heirs, though, for the charter then states that his widow and son then carried out a raid of their own, killing seventeen people and seizing an estate at Bourne.[79]

Wulfbold's actions grew out of an inheritance dispute, but most cases of this sort were resolved with far less violence. Lawmakers went to great lengths to protect the rights of heirs and ensure that disputes would be settled by law rather than bloodshed. *I Edward* (c. 900 × 925), for example, is one of several law codes to penalize the withholding of estates granted by bequest, and *III Æthelred* (c. 997) protects heirs from posthumous lawsuits brought against the deceased. Likewise, *II Cnut* decrees that the heirs of a man who died in battle shall be guaranteed their inheritance.[80] Judging from surviving records, disputes over inheritance were relatively common during this period. The dispute between Wynflæd and Leofwine concerned inherited land, while the outlawing of the widow's son in the dispute that began this section most likely reflects an effort to ensure that he could not claim his rights as heir to any of the Ailsworth estates. One of the most detailed accounts of an inheritance dispute occurs in a charter issued by Eadgifu, third wife of Edward the Elder, whose own inheritance was wrongfully seized:

> Þa Eadred geendude 7 man Eadgife berypte ælcere are, þa namon Godan twegen suna, Leofstan 7 Leofric, on Eadgife þas twa forespecenen land æt Culingon 7 æt Osterlande. 7 sædon þam cilde Eadwige þe þa gecoren wæs þæt hy rihtur hiora wæren þonne hire. Þæt þa swa wæs oþ Eadgar astiþude. 7 he 7 his wytan gerehton þæt hy manfull reaflac gedon hæfden, 7 hi hire hire are gerehton 7 agefon.

> When Eadred died and Eadgifu was robbed of all her property, two of Goda's sons, Leofstan and Leofric, seized from Eadgifu the two previously mentioned estates at Cooling and Osterland. And they told young Eadwige, who had just been named king, that their claim was more just than hers. That is how things stood until Edward ascended the throne. Then he and his councilors ruled that they had committed a shameful theft and they adjudged the property hers and gave it to her.[81]

Eadgifu's lawsuit highlights the fact that high status was no protection against the unscrupulous. More importantly, this text, along with the charters featuring Wynflæd and the Ailsworth widow, also reflects women's heightened vulnerability to land seizures of this sort. In many cases, women did not hold land

---

[79] S 877, ed. Miller, *Charters of New Minster*, no. 31, pp. 207–209. See also Rabin, "Capital Punishment," 193–99.

[80] *I Edward* 2, *III Æthelred* 14, and *II Cnut* 78.

[81] S 1211, ed. Brooks and Kelly, *Charters of Christ Church Canterbury*, no. 124, vol. II, pp. 958–63.

outright, but instead held it in usufruct: they had use of the land during their lifetime or until their children grew to adulthood, but could not sell it or bequeath it in their own right. Although women were not without legal recourse (as will be discussed in more detail in section 4), their ability to assert claims to landed property often failed without the intervention of a male ally or protector. In the absence of such an advocate, the female claimant could well suffer the fate of the Ailsworth widow: expulsion and dispossession.

A final type of property vulnerable to theft were slaves, who occupied an uneasy middle ground between chattel and full legal personhood.[82] An individual might be enslaved for a variety of reasons: one could be born a slave, captured during a raid or battle, sentenced to slavery for a serious legal offense, or compelled to enter slavery to pay off a debt. The enslaved were not wholly without rights – they were to be granted time for religious observance, for example, and could receive support from the church if impoverished – but they were nonetheless subject to the will and whims of their owners. In contrast to the free population, slaves suffered more severe penalties for wrongdoing and received little or no compensation if wronged themselves. The laws of Æthelstan, for instance, ruled that slaves guilty of theft were to be stoned to death, while the laws of Cnut allow a slave to escape a first conviction for theft with only a branding, but at the second conviction "ne sy ðær nan bot buton þæt heafod" (there can be no penalty except [the slave's] head).[83] The potential for culpability and right to compensation, however small, indicates at least some recognition of slaves' personhood (albeit of the lowest status); yet this recognition does not detract from their treatment as commodities to be bought, sold, and used at their owner's discretion. Insofar as they were understood to be property, the trafficking of slaves was strictly regulated and their theft severely punished. Thus, the treaty between King Alfred and the Viking leader Guthrum grouped slaves with horses and oxen as commodities requiring a warranty that they had not been stolen from their previous owners. The treaty also forbade the selling of English slaves to Danish owners and vice versa.[84] The reasoning behind the prohibition can be found in the law code *V Æthelred*, which decrees that "man Cristene men 7 unforworhte of earde ne sylle, ne huru on hæðene þeode, ac beorge georne þæt man þa sawla ne forfare þe Crist mid his agenum life gebohte" (those who are Christian and free of guilt shall not be sold out of this land, and especially not to heathen people; but we must zealously ensure that the souls not be destroyed which Christ purchased with his own life).[85]

---

[82] Pelteret, *Slavery*, 241–51; Jurasinski, *Old English Penitentials,* 95–100; Rio, *Slavery*, esp. 67–70.

[83] *IV Æthelstan* 6.7 and *II Cnut* 32–32.1.   [84] *Alfred-Guthrum* 4–5.

[85] *V Æthelred* 2. See Jurasinski, *Old English Penitentials,* 112–17.

V Æthelred's concern with the state of the slave's soul should not be taken too far, though: the largest collection of royal manumissions, the so-called Bodmin Manumissions preserved in the manuscript London, British Library Additional 9381, records that multiple slaves were granted their freedom by nearly every ruler from Edmund forward. Æthelred, though, freed only one.

3.1.2 Offenses Against Persons

Perhaps the most well-known passages in the laws of Æthelbert and Alfred are the lengthy series of clauses setting out the penalties for injury to various parts of the body.[86] In their specificity, the injury schedules testify to a precise understanding of the body's anatomy as well as the consequences should it be damaged. Not surprisingly, the determination of penalty rests in large part on functionality. *Æthelbert*, for instance, distinguishes between the fine for the loss of an ear (twelve shillings), the piercing of an ear (three shillings), the laceration of an ear (six shillings), and the loss of hearing in an ear (twenty-five shillings).[87] Similarly, *Alfred* assigns a particularly high penalty (eighty shillings) for damage to testicles so severe as to prevent the victim from fathering children. (For the sake of comparison, it should be noted that this fine is equal to that of the loss of an arm.)[88] Also important are injuries that affect the victim's looks: *Æthelbert* penalizes a bruise to a part of the body covered by clothing less (twenty *sceattas*) than it does a bruise on an uncovered part of the body (thirty *sceattas*), while *Alfred* sets a lower fine for an inch-long wound under the hair (one shilling) than it does for an inch-long wound outside the hair (two shillings).[89] The degree of detail in these clauses suggests that the injury schedules may have been compiled as much to provide test cases for legal guidance as they were to address specific acts of violence. Thus, *Alfred*'s distinctions between fractured ribs that break the skin and those that do not or its doubling of penalties for wounds before the hairline, below the sleeve, and beneath the knee provide useful rubrics for assessing the severity of injuries beyond those specified in the text.

The injury schedules are hardly the only references to bodily harm in royal legislation: *Hlothhere and Eadric* sets a specific penalty for injuries caused because of drunkenness; *III Edmund* legislates against attacks committed by escaped slaves; and *II Cnut* penalizes violence towards the clergy, to cite three examples.[90] Unsurprisingly, however, the act of violence that most occupied

---

[86] *Æthelbert* 33–73 and *Alfred* 44–77. For a comprehensive discussion of the injury schedules, see Oliver, *The Body Legal in Barbarian Law*.

[87] *Æthelbert* 39–42.   [88] *Alfred* 65–66. Oliver, "Genital Mutilation."

[89] *Æthelbert* 59–60 and *Alfred* 45–45.1.

[90] *Hlothhere and Eadric* 12–14, *III Edmund* 4, and *II Cnut* 39.

early English lawmakers was homicide, though the penalty could vary widely depending on the circumstances and the victim. The laws of Æthelberht, for example, established set fines to be paid if a person was slain on royal property and if the victim was a member of the king's household, with higher penalties reserved for servants of higher rank. *Æthelberht* also set specific penalties for killing the free and the unfree as well as their dependents. Significantly, it appears that the majority of these fines were owed to the king for the violation of his "drihtenbeag" (lordly rights) rather than to the victim's family as compensation for the loss of a loved one.[91] Æthelberht and his successors also recognized finer distinctions, such as the penalty for committing murder with borrowed weapons yet without the owner's consent; for killing a thief; for killing a foreigner; for a murder committed by a Welshman; for killing a pregnant woman or the child of a nun; for the murder of a dependent by his guardian; for a murder committed by someone without relatives to pay compensation; for a murder committed by a priest; for the killing of another's slaves; and for killings committed unintentionally, just to name a few.[92] The care taken to distinguish between different kinds of violent death indicates legislators' concern to stem retaliatory acts that might disrupt the public peace. In doing so, though, they also provided a regulatory index to the perceived value of the different ranks within pre-Conquest society. This value is reflected not just in fines owed to the king but also in the different rates of *wergild* (the monetary compensation to be paid in cases of violent death) owed to the victim's family.

Rape and other forms of sexual assault occupy a special category in pre-Conquest law. Royal legislation penalizes a wide array of sexual offenses, though these penalties are often more valuable for the light they shed on the gendered nature of early English law than for the list of offenses they regulate.[93] Unlike theft or homicide, sexual assault is punished only with a financial penalty, typically related to the status of the victim. Assaults against minors, unmarried women, widows and women in holy orders were penalized more severely, while the fines for assaulting slaves or serving women were relatively light. Although earlier legislation does not specify who should receive the fine, later laws decree that it is to be paid to the king, church, or closest male relative rather than to the victim.[94] In identifying male authority figures as the proper recipients of compensation, the laws indicate the type of offense sexual assault

---

[91] *Æthelberht* 5, 6, 7, 12, 21, 25, 26.

[92] See, for instance, *Æthelberht* 20; *Wihtred* 25; *Ine* 23–23.1 and 74; *Alfred* 8.3, 13, 17, and 30.1.

[93] For a more comprehensive discussion, see Coleman, "Rape in Anglo-Saxon England," 193–204 and Horner, "The Language of Rape," 149–83.

[94] See *Alfred* 8, *Alfred* 18, *I Edmund* 4, *VI Æthelred* 12.1, *VI Æthelred* 39, *I Cnut* 7.1, and *Cnut 1020* 16.

was thought to be: while modern legislation treats sexual assault as an attack on the rights and person of the victim, pre-Conquest law characterized it as a violation of the protection extended to the woman by the crown, church, or her family. It was an offense against their authority more than her person. Viewed in this context, the threat posed by sexual assault was not merely its violence against the peace of the kingdom or the safety of the homestead; rather, the greater concern was the threat it posed to traditional patterns of land tenure. The difficulty in establishing paternity in an age before genetic testing meant that any act that introduced ambiguity into the clear line of paternal descent raised the specter of family property passing into the hands of someone outside the bloodline. The anxiety provoked by the threat of wrongful inheritance explains why women suffered more serious penalties for wrongful sexual behavior than did men: *II Cnut*, for instance, states that a man guilty of rape or adultery merely has to pay a financial penalty while an adulterous woman was punished with the confiscation of all her possessions and the loss of her nose and ears.[95] In effect, her willingness to endanger her family's inheritance through improper sexual activity resulted in disfigurement severe enough to permanently make known her dishonor and visible enough to eliminate any future prospect of a husband or a lover.

Beyond specific crimes against an individual, the greatest potential for physical harm likely occurred during periodic feuds between families or communities. Indeed, the threat of feud was considered sufficiently serious to inspire repeated attempts at regulation in royal law codes. *Alfred*, for instance, decrees that disputants must seek arbitration before resorting to violence and that an accuser cannot lay siege to his adversary's home for more than seven days. If, once this time has elapsed, the accused leaves the house unarmed, the accuser must bring him to court rather than executing summary justice.[96]

Although attempts to legislate against feuds were relatively frequent under royal law, it is not entirely certain that those pursuing vendettas necessarily understood themselves to be participating in extra-legal activity. One tenth-century charter documenting a decade-long feud over the Middlesex estates of Sunbury and Send records the participants engaging in abduction, property seizure, the withholding of compensation, rebellion, and the refusal to turn fines and property over to the king. However, the length of the dispute was such that it encompassed the reigns of three kings – Eadred, Eadwig, and Edgar. In the words of the charter, with each change of government "wendun gewyrda"

---

[95] *II Cnut* 50–54.

[96] *Alfred* 5 and 42–42.7. For a broader discussion of feud's place in early English law, see Fletcher, *Bloodfeud*; Hyams, "Feud and the State," 1–43; Hyams, *Rancor and Reconciliation*, 78–87; and Lambert, *Law and Order*, especially 163–202.

(fortune changed) also, so that the faction considered to have the more lawful claim changed as well. Ultimately, the dispute only ended when one of the claimants died in possession of the estates and willed them to Archbishop Dunstan of Canterbury. Edgar then confiscated the estates as the property of a traitor and granted them to one of his followers, from whom Dunstan was finally able to purchase them.[97] The legal muddle surrounding the Sunbury and Send estates reflects the fact that the line between legal action and extra-legal violence was seldom clear. Strategies, lawful or unlawful, were chosen for their effectiveness rather than their legality. More importantly, the repeated reversals of fortune illustrate the extent to which the "lawfulness" of action in a feud or dispute could depend more on political patronage that on a strict reading of formal legislation. Today's law could easily become tomorrow's crime.

3.1.3 Offenses Against Authority

Within the political hierarchy of pre-Conquest England, the highest stratum of authority was occupied by the closely related institutions of king and church. Although frequently at odds, the crown and church shared many of the same legal interests and priorities. Accordingly, offenses against the one often closely echoed offenses against the other. The many similarities between the secular and spiritual powers make it possible to divide violations against their authority into three principal categories: violations of space, violations of fidelity, and violations of prerogatives.

Among the most visible signs of royal and ecclesiastical authority was the definition of their immediate vicinity as a sacrosanct space with heightened legal protections and obligations. In the case of the king, the space of royal authority can be imagined as a series of concentric circles, each narrower than the last. In its broadest sense, the entire kingdom was under the crown's authority, so any violation of the public peace was not only an injury to the victim, but also an attack on the king's rights as ruler and protector. Thus, the earliest surviving text of royal law, the legislation of Æthelberht, characterizes the act of homicide as an infringement upon the king's "drihtenbeag" (lordly rights), while the latest, *II Cnut*, establishes set fines to be paid by malefactors for their violation of the protection (*mund*) extended by the king to his kingdom.[98] Within this category also fell the king's jurisdictional rights, expressed in the series of formulaic pairings *sac and soc*, *toll and team*, and *infangthief and outfangthief*. The first of these is the right to hold a court; the second permits a landowner to collect a fee on all commercial activities

---

[97] S 1447, ed. Robertson, *Anglo-Saxon Charters*, no. 44, pp. 90–93.
[98] *Æthelberht* 6 and *II Cnut* 12 and 42.

taking place on his property as well as the right to hold a court for the resolution of financial disputes and to benefit from its profits; and the third is the right of a lord to execute summary justice on any criminal caught on his property. Although in many cases these rights were held by local lords as the result of longstanding local practice, the king's authority to grant or revoke such rights suggests that jurisdiction was ultimately held by the crown. (Of course, the question of whether individual kings possessed enough political capital to assert these rights is another matter entirely.) More narrowly, there was the specific jurisdiction the king held over his agents. For instance, *III Edgar* penalizes the judge "þe oðrum woh deme" (who passes wrongful judgment on another) and *III Æthelred* decrees that, "nan man nage nane socne ofer cynges þegen buton cyng sylf" (none shall have jurisdiction over a king's thegn except the king himself).[99] Most severely punished, however, were violations, especially violent ones, committed in the immediate vicinity of the king. Penalties were assessed for fighting in the king's presence, drawing weapons in the king's hall, and committing theft or homicide on the king's property. These laws were not always successful, though, as the assassination of King Edmund by a thief during a feast at Pucklechurch illustrates. Nonetheless, they do reflect a concerted royal strategy to express the authority of the king and to make manifest his power, even in his absence, over the whole of the kingdom.

The church likewise sought to exercise its authority, both spiritual and legal, through claims of protection and jurisdiction. In its broadest sense, ecclesiastical jurisdiction, much like royal protection, encompassed the entire kingdom. Beginning with the laws of Wihtred, it became common practice for the church to employ secular legislation for the enforcement of religious doctrine.[100] The laws of Alfred, for instance, penalized those who contravened church law (*halig ryht*) during Lent and, at least from the reign of Edgar, bishops sat alongside regional *ealdormen* as judges over local courts.[101] Although the degree to which royal and ecclesiastical jurisdiction differed from one another during this period remains a subject of some dispute, violations against church property and personnel rated more severe penalties than did offenses against their secular counterparts. *Æthelberht* decrees that theft from a priest must be compensated at nine times the cost of the stolen items while *VIII Æthelred* (c. 1014) straightforwardly declares that "weofodþena mæðe medemige man for Godes ege" (the status of those who serve at the altar is to be respected for fear of God).[102] Most important, however, was the inviolability of churches and their property. In many cases, prohibitions concerning churches look much the same as those

---

[99] *III Edgar* 3 and *III Æthelred* 11   [100] Oliver, "Royal and Ecclesiastical Law," 25–44.
[101] *Alfred* 40.2 and *III Edgar* 5.2. See Marafioti, "Crime and Sin," 59–84.
[102] *Æthelberht* 1 and *VIII Æthelred* 18

concerning the royal presence: the bearing of weapons is forbidden and special penalties are assessed for acts of murder, assault, and theft. Yet, above all of these is the church's right of sanctuary.[103] Although the church's prerogative to offer sanctuary is present as far back as the laws of Æthelberht and Alfred, it became a special priority in the laws of Æthelred and Cnut drafted by Archbishop Wulfstan of York. In *VIII Æthelred* he established a schedule of penalties for violations of sanctuary at a cathedral (a fine equivalent to the king's *wergild*) all the way down to infringing upon the protection of a country chapel (thirty shillings), for though "Ne syn ealle cyrcan na gelicre mæðe worldlice wirð, þeah hi godcundlice habban halgunge gelice" (not all churches are equal in status under the law, yet spiritually they all hold equal holiness).[104] Even more forceful is his declaration in *I Cnut* that "Ælc cyrice is mid rihte on Cristes agenan griðe 7 ælc Christen man ah mycele þearfe þæt he on þam griðe mycele mæðe wite, forðam Godes grið is ealra griða selost to geearnigenne 7 geornost to healdenne, 7 þær nehst cininges" (Each church is by right under the protection of Christ himself, and every Christian has a great duty to act with utmost respect for that protection, for of all forms of protection, the protection of God is to be most sought after and most diligently upheld, and after that the king's).[105] For Wulfstan, the church's right to offer sanctuary marked the boundary at which secular law ended. The sacredness of the church's precincts – including not just the building itself but the immediate land around it – superseded even the jurisdiction of the king. Here the law of God could not be challenged.

The spatial focus of so much early English law reflects the recognition that political power rested upon the assertion of jurisdiction, whether by the earthly king or the heavenly one. Equally important to crown and church, though, was the prerogative to command the fidelity of those within their jurisdiction. For the king, this entailed framing ritualized oathtaking as the central act of a loyal subject. It is difficult to overstate the importance of the oath in pre-Conquest society.[106] *Swerian*, an oath formulary of the mid-tenth century, includes oaths of allegiance, oaths of accusation and defense, oaths of witnessing and suretyship, and oaths for use in the pedestrian business of everyday life. The clause that opens the laws of Alfred states in no uncertain terms that it is of "mæst ðearf " (utmost importance) that every person "að 7 his wed wærlice healde" (diligently keep his oath and pledge), a sentiment echoed in either phrasing or substance in nearly all subsequent law codes.[107] *II Cnut* further decrees that

---

[103] Shoemaker, *Sanctuary and Crime*, 47–90.   [104] *VIII Æthelred* 5–5.1   [105] *I Cnut* 2.1.
[106] Matthias Ammon, "The Functions of Oath and Pledge," 515–35, and Hudson, *Oxford History*, 81–84.
[107] *Alfred* 1.

every boy over the age of twelve must swear to abide by the law upon being recognized as an adult by the regional court.[108] The king and his agents were assiduous in making certain that his subjects' oaths were kept: in addition to pledging their loyalty, men were also to appoint ten "sureties," respected members of the community whose job it was to ensure that the oathtaker fulfilled his oath.[109] The emphasis on oathtaking can also be found in the charters, which record the swearing of numerous oaths as well as disputes decided by which claimant is deemed "*aðe ðæs ðe near* " (nearer the oath).[110]

Given the significance of oaths within pre-Conquest culture, it can be no surprise that perjury was condemned with equal vigor. The swearing of false oaths was considered such a significant crime that the laws of Hlothhere and Eadric state that anyone who accuses someone of perjury in another's house is to pay a fine to the person accused, the owner of the house, and the king.[111] *Alfred* rules that those who fail to fulfill their oaths must give their weapons and possessions to their family before being imprisoned for forty days. *Alfred* further states that those whose oath of loyalty to their lord proves false – whether commoner or aristocrat – are to be executed and all their possessions forfeit.[112] *II Æthelstan*, with characteristic severity, forbids those who swear falsely from taking oaths in the future and decrees that they may not be buried in sacred ground.[113] *I Edmund* links perjury to sorcery (*liblac*) and declares that those guilty of either crime are to be excommunicated.[114] *VI Æthelred* (c. 1008) forbids perjurers from entering into the presence of the king, while *II Cnut* orders that those who swear a false oath over holy relics are to lose their hand and forfeit half of their property.[115] In addition, those considered not oath-worthy – that is, those previously convicted of perjury or, even if never the subject of a criminal complaint, are deemed untrustworthy by the community – require additional proof if accused of wrongdoing and must have a surety to oversee their actions to ensure that they continue to obey the law. The ubiquity of oathtaking (and oathbreaking) clauses in royal legislation suggests something of their importance to kings seeking to consolidate and centralize the governance of their kingdom: although the majority of people may never have seen the king or stood in his presence, oathtaking rituals provided a symbolic point of contact between the individual and the royal court. Even if the king could exert only limited authority in communities too distant or too independent to recognize his authority, the swearing of oaths ensured that each person nonetheless recognized themselves as his subject.

---

[108] *II Cnut* 21.   [109] See *III Edgar* 6, *IV Edgar* 3, I *Æthelred* 1, and *II Cnut* 20.

[110] S 1445. See section 4. A Latin rendering of the phrase also occurs in the twelfth-century *Liber Eliensis*, II.25.

[111] *Hlothhere and Eadric* 11.   [112] *Alfred* 1.2 and 4–4.2.   [113] *II Æthelstan* 26.

[114] *I Edmund* 6.   [115] *VI Æthelred* 36 and *II Cnut* 36–36.1.

Regarding the church, it is in the nature of the institution to demand the fidelity of its adherents. Yet characterizing that fidelity as a legal obligation allowed the church to treat violations of faith as a danger to public wellbeing no less perilous than the threat they posed to individual salvation. This link between Christian faith and the welfare of king and kingdom is emphasized in the first clause of *I Cnut*: "Ðæt is þonne ærest: þæt hi ofer ealle oþre þingc ænne God æfre woldan lufian 7 wurþian 7 ænne Cristendom anrædlice healdan and Cnut cingc lufian mid rihtan getrywþan" (This is foremost: that above all [the people] always love and worship the one God and constantly uphold the one Christian faith and obey King Cnut with proper fidelity).[116] Faithful adherence to Christian doctrine thus became a crucial factor in ensuring political stability. Violations of faith, however, endangered that stability. *IV Edgar*, for instance, attributes a widespread plague to "synnum 7 mid oferhyrnysse Godes beboda" (sin and the neglect of God's laws).[117] Likewise, the law code *VII Æthelred*, issued in response to the Viking invasion of 1009, calls for kingdomwide penance in order to purge the realm of the sins that brought on the invasion. The decree calls for three days of fasting and penance, during which each adult Christian is to, "ad confessionem vadat et nudis pedibus ad ecclesiam et peccatis omnibus abrenuntiet" (go to confession and, with bare feet, to church, and by renouncing his sins, mend his ways and cease from them).[118] The link between law and morality operated on an individual level as well. In some cases, moral and legal violations were one and the same, as in the law codes' frequent identification of perjury with the biblical injunction against bearing false witness. More broadly, *V Æthelred* decrees that each of his subjects must "gime his Cristendomes georne 7 gewunige gelomlice to scrifte 7 unforwandodlice his synna gecyðe" (zealously adhere to their Christian faith and go frequently to confession, and openly confess their sins). Failure to do so could result in the malefactor being declared an apostate (*wiðersacan*) and sentenced to both excommunication and exile.[119] In other words, to commit an offense against the church is to provoke the wrath of both God and government.

In commanding the fidelity of their followers, both king and church developed rituals designed to give abstractions such as faith and loyalty a tangible reality to those within their jurisdiction. In doing so, they also provided an ideological justification for the more specific material obligations they demanded of their subjects and the severe penalties assessed when those obligations were not met. For the king, these duties took three primary forms: financial, infrastructural, and military.[120] A crucial component of royal attempts

---

[116] *I Cnut* 1.   [117] *IV Edgar* 1.   [118] *VII Æthelred* 2–2.1.   [119] *V Æthelred* 22.
[120] Abels, *Lordship and Military Obligation*, 97–115.

to centralize governance was the issuance of decrees designed to regularize coinage.[121] Not only was the minting of currency a strictly controlled privilege limited only to those with a royal warrant, but those convicted of producing unauthorized coinage were subject to penalties ranging from the loss of a hand to the loss of life.[122] Controlling the circulation of money facilitated royal enforcement of pre-Conquest England's complex tax structure. The king held the right to impose taxes on land, servant labor, travel on his highways, commercial transactions, foreign commodities, and the profits generated by regional courts. It was also within the king's authority to impose specific dues to support the church, military endeavors (*heregeld*), ad hoc needs (*gafol*), or in Æthelred's case, the payment of tribute (*Danegeld*). In addition, he could collect *heriot*, an inheritance tax payable in money, livestock, or weapons originally held from the deceased's lord. Failure to pay one's taxes could result in the loss of some or all of the delinquent's property, confinement or, in extreme cases, outlawry.[123] As no taxation rolls survive from the period, we cannot tell how the king's exactions were received, but there is little reason to think that they were any less harsh than those of other early medieval rulers. In addition to financial obligations, the king also commanded that wealthy landowners and regional lords oversee the upkeep of the public infrastructure within their demesne. Particularly important was their duty to pay for the maintenance of fortifications and bridges (*burhbot 7 bricbot*).[124] Decrees of this sort became increasingly common in the tenth century as the continuation of Viking hostility meant that system of burghs established by Alfred remained central to the kingdom's defense. Finally, the king had the right to command military service from regional hundreds, lords and their dependents (who often held land in exchange for service), and those who held land directly from the crown. This pattern of obligation indicates that, more than land distribution, lordship was the principal factor in determining military service. As a result, those who refused to serve violated their obligations to their lord, king, and kingdom. Within this context, it makes sense that delinquents in military service were punished in much the same way as those who refused to pay their taxes: ruinous fines and the forfeiture of most or all of the recusant's property.[125]

Royal taxes were only one type of exaction the inhabitants of pre-Conquest England were expected to pay. The church levied its own dues as well. Timed to coincide with the liturgical calendar, the church collected a tithe on arable land fifteen days after Easter, a tithe on young animals at Pentecost, a tithe on the

---

[121] Naismith, *Money and Power*, 156–57.

[122] *III Æthelred* 16 and *V Æthelred* 5.3. See Screen, "Numismatics."

[123] Carella, "Earliest Expression," 111–43.   [124] See, for instance, *II Cnut* 10 and 65.

[125] Abels, *Lordship and Military Obligation*, 94–95.

harvest at All Saints. Dues owed to Rome were collected on the feast of St. Peter and those for the upkeep of the church on Martinmas. Money to pay for the lighting of the church was to be paid on Easter, All Saints, and Candlemas. Those who had a church on their property were also responsible for a further set of dues, the amount of which increased if it possessed a cemetery. Finally, dues for the soul of a deceased relative were to be paid before the grave was closed.[126] Refusal to render one's contribution resulted in fines, mandatory penance, excommunication, and the forfeiture of property, which was divided between church and King. The forms that church dues took are not particularly surprising; however, more striking is the full integration of tithes and other ecclesiastical exactions into royal law and the division of penalties between church and King. To offend the church thus became little different than challenging the authority of the king himself.

3.2 Who were the Offenders?

The limited documentary record leaves us no way to tally the number of crimes committed in early medieval England nor have we the means to profile their perpetrators; however, surviving legal texts do provide at least some sense of those who were believed most likely to commit illegal acts as well as the extent to which different categories of people could be held responsible for wrongful acts. Measuring degrees of culpability is not simply an exercise in comparison, however. Culpability infers that the perpetrator not only committed an illegal act, but also that they were aware of its illegality while committing it. The measure of culpability is also the measure of capacity. In other words, the more liable a malefactor is held to be, the more that person is recognized to be a fully realized subject of the law. Likewise, the greater the expectation that a class of individuals will commit a violation, the lower that class will fall in Anglo-Saxon evaluations of social status. And, perhaps most importantly, as the example at the head of this section illustrates, the stronger the hold that these expectations have on a community, the more useful they become in conjuring a perception of wrongful behavior where none may exist.

Those whose status served as the greatest mitigating factor were children and the infirm.[127] The laws of Ine place the lowest limit of culpability at ten; however, presumably because of his limited understanding and the outsized influence of his parents, at this age a child can only be treated as an accessory to theft rather than the perpetrator.[128] More harshly, the laws of Æthelstan decree

---

[126] *I Cnut* 8–14.

[127] On the laws concerning the potential culpability of children, the infirm, and women, see Rabin, "Parent-Child Litigation," 270–90.

[128] *Ine* 7.2.

that a child can be hanged for theft at twelve, though this clause appears to have been the subject of some controversy as the king later raised the age to fifteen, apparently at the behest of the archbishop of Canterbury and the bishop of London.[129] Prior to reaching an age of understanding, culpability lay with the child's parents rather the child himself, a practice followed in the case of the disabled as well. The laws of Alfred, for instance, grant immunity from prosecution to the deaf and those unable to speak, instead ascribing responsibility for their actions to their fathers. It seems unlikely, though, that Alfred intended to limit legal protections only to individuals with these particular disabilities, for he also adds the stipulation that those with legal immunity must be unable to "synna onsecggan ne geandettan" (deny nor admit [their] misdeeds).[130] A lack of comprehension, more than just a physical impairment, appears to be the primary factor in assigning culpability. That said, grounding guilt in understanding is not merely an acknowledgement that children and individuals with a serious disability were unable to take full responsibility for their actions: it also serves as a form of protection against those who would capitalize on this vulnerability for their own gain. Indeed, manufacturing guilt appears to have been quite a profitable business in pre-Conquest England. Because a convict's property was typically subject to seizure – as was the case with the Ailsworth widow – accusations against those incapable of mounting a meaningful defense could serve as a means of acquiring property. It is to this practice *II Cnut* refers when it complains that "Hit wæs ær ðysson þæt þæt cild ðe læg on ðam cradol, þeah hit næfre metes ne abite, þæt ða gytseras lætan ealswascyldigne 7 hit gewittig wære" (hitherto it has been common for avaricious persons to treat as a child that lays in the cradle, one who has never tasted food, as if it were as culpable as one with full understanding).[131] Clauses such as this are a useful reminder of early law's focus on the prevention of property theft, particularly in cases that would disrupt patterns of land tenure and inheritance. The circumstances addressed by *II Cnut* were concerned with the latter: the grasping litigant not merely taking candy from a baby, but also threatening the proper descent of a family's patrimonial holdings. Within this context, the immunities and protections of those without the means to fully comprehend the law may have been a means of protecting the most vulnerable, but they had significant consequences for the future of the community as well.

The status of women in this regard is considerably more complex. On one hand, the laws held that a woman committing wrongful acts on her own or in concert with her husband should be held culpable to the same degree as would a man in an identical situation. On the other hand, though, legislation

---

[129] *VI Æthelstan* 12.1.   [130] *Alfred* 14.   [131] *II Cnut* 76.2.

concerning criminal culpability also recognized the limitations placed on a woman's agency by the male head of household or, in monastic life, the diocese's bishop. Thus, the laws of Wihtred exonerated a wife if her husband had engaged in devil worship without her knowledge.[132] Likewise, the contemporary laws of Ine made a similar stipulation regarding a wife's ignorance of thefts committed by her husband, adding also that she could not be considered an accomplice unless she made use of the stolen goods for "hio sceal hire ealdore hieran" (a woman must obey her husband).[133] Æthelstan, otherwise known for the severity of his laws, made provision for the wife of a husband who committed wrongful acts without her knowledge.[134] In a similar vein, *II Cnut* absolves a wife of her husband's thefts unless the stolen goods are found in the storeroom, her chest, or her cupboard – spaces considered properly hers to oversee and to which she has the key – in which case she is to be treated as an accomplice. Yet even in this situation, the laws, echoing *Ine*, acknowledge that "ne mæg nan wif hire bundan forbeodan þæt he ne mote into his cotan gelegian þæt þæt he wille" (a wife cannot prevent her husband from bringing whatever he likes into his house).[135] Evidence of the attenuated nature of women's agency can be found in other legal documents as well, perhaps most vividly in a charter recording the history of a series of disputed estates at Bromley and Fawkham in Kent. Although the disposition of the properties had been negotiated by their original owner Ælfric, after his death "ongan ða syððan Brihtric ðære wydewan mæg 7 heo to ðam genedde þæt hy brucan ðara landa on reaflace" (the widow's kinsman Brihtric intervened and forced her to recover the lands by violence).[136] Episodes of this sort highlight women's middling place in the pre-Conquest legal hierarchy. They were recognized – and in cases of wrongdoing, penalized – as autonomous adults fully responsible for their actions; however, they were also subordinate to the guardianship and undue influence of their male relatives. In a sense, they occupied the ambiguous border that separates child from adult: agentive in some cases, subject in others.

Although women, children, the infirm, and the stranger all might be described as marginal figures in early English law, individuals in more powerful positions also attracted suspicion, most frequently the reeve. As the individual in a community tasked with enforcing the laws of lord and king, the local reeve collected taxes and fees, participated in the adjudication of disputes, and represented the interests of the aristocracy to those lower down on the social scale. Within his jurisdiction, the reeve could easily become a target of bitterness: for those frustrated with the policies of royal or local government, the

---

[132] *Wihtred* 12.   [133] *Ine* 7.1.   [134] *IV Æthelstan* 3.   [135] *II Cnut* 76.1.
[136] S 1457, ed. Campbell, *Charters of* Rochester, no. 29, pp. 34–36.

reeve's proximity made it easier to direct blame at him rather than a more distant figure of authority. Moreover, the various legal roles entrusted to him – especially those with potential financial benefit – invited accusations of corruption, many of which were doubtless justified. The increasingly severe penalties for dishonest reeves from their first appearance in the laws of Æthelred to their last in the laws of Cnut suggest that corruption among government officers was a constant problem in the pre-Conquest state. From the king's perspective, a reeve's most serious offense was permitting (or at least overlooking) the minting of false coins in his jurisdiction, for which he was to receive the same punishment as the counterfeiter, the loss of his hand.[137] Accusations of wrongdoing can be found in other genres of texts as well: the corrupt reeve is a stock figure in early medieval English hagiography, in which he is depicted as a dishonest administrator eager to test his own power against that of the saint.[138] Likewise, in the *Institutes of Polity*, Archbishop Wulfstan rails that, "þæt ma is þæra rypera þonne rihtwisra, and is earmlic ðing þæt ða syndon ryperas þe sceoldan beon hyrdas Cristenes folces. Hy rypað þa earman butan ælcere scylde oðre hwile and hynað þa heorde, þe hi sceoldan healdan, and mid yfelan holan earme men beswicað, and unlaga rærað on æghwylce wisan earmum to hynþe and wydewan bestrypað oft and gelome" (it is a terrible thing that they are thieves who should be the shepherds of the Christian people. At times, they steal from those who are poor through no fault of their own and torment the flock which they should protect, and abuse the unfortunate with evil slander, and promote unjust laws in every way to exploit the needy and rob widows again and again).[139] Little evidence survives for the political views of those in the middle or lower strata of early English society, yet the many references to reeves' suspect behavior suggest that their role may have been a point of tension in pre-Conquest communities. It also suggests that at least some of those suspicions may have been justified.

It has been suggested by historians of more recent law that early medieval England lacked a concept of jurisprudence, yet this accusation is as inaccurate as it is unfair. Although the means of categorizing legal offenses differed significantly from those used in a modern courtroom, they nonetheless reflect a sophisticated understanding of wrongdoing that indicates awareness of its causes, a hierarchy of severity distinguishing the more serious crimes from the more trivial, and a consideration of those factors that might either mitigate or exacerbate guilt. It was also equally given to corruption by those in a position to bend its rules and manipulate its practices, as the Ailsworth widow and her family found to their detriment. Yet concepts of wrongdoing give us only half

---

[137] *IV Æthelred* 7.3 and *II Cnut* 8.2.   [138] See section 4.2.   [139] *Institutes of Polity* 10.

the picture. Equally important were the means by which the law was enforced and its violators tried and punished.

4 Enforcing the Law

The earliest letter from a commoner to the king survives in the form of a petition submitted to Edward the Elder concerning events that had taken place during the reign of his father, Alfred. The author of the petition is unnamed, though the most likely candidate is the West Saxon *ealdorman* Ordlaf, within whose jurisdiction the events described in the letter took place. The text concerns the misdeeds of a singularly unsuccessful thief named Helmstan, an apparently wealthy (if larcenous) landowner and godson to the letter's author. Having been caught attempting to steal a belt, Helmstan's resulting status as a known thief cost him his ability to defend himself in court, a vulnerability exploited by one of his neighbors, Æthelm Higa, who attempted to claim several of his estates. Helmstan sought the help of his godfather Ordlaf, who interceded with King Alfred to restore the legal privileges of the newly penitent thief. Helmstan was thus able to defend his ownership of the lands before the local court, conveniently overseen by Ordlaf himself. Although initially victorious in defending his property rights, Helmstan's subsequent (failed) attempt to steal a herd of cattle led to the final confiscation of his lands and left him once more without legal privileges. Having taken over Helmstan's property, Ordlaf exchanged it with the bishop of Winchester for estates of equivalent value. Undeterred, Æthelm Higa renewed his claim, and so Ordlaf petitioned King Edward to dismiss Higa's claim once and for all. His attempt appears to have been successful as a note on the letter's dorse records that Æthelm Higa withdrew his suit.[140]

The significance of the Fonthill Letter lies in its extraordinary detail. Few other pre-Conquest documents record the consequences of legal wrongdoing and the progress of an extended property dispute in such specific terms. Yet the text raises as many problems as it solves. Although the detailed narrative conveys the impression of objectivity, it nonetheless reflects the perspective and legal agenda of Ordlaf, who omits any evidence that Æthelm Higa might have had to support his claim and whose canny exchange of lands with the bishop of Winchester required Higa to challenge the power and prerogatives of the church, rather than the property rights of a mere *ealdorman*. Perhaps more striking is the extent to which the responses to Helmstan's crimes and Higa's claims are determined by networks of family influence and political patronage.

---

[140] S 1445. The Fonthill Letter has been edited in Brooks and Kelly, *Charters of Christ Church, Canterbury*, no. 104, vol. II, 852–54. Useful discussions of its contents can be found there as well as in Brooks, "Fonthill Letter," 301–318; Keynes, "Fonthill Letter," 53–97; and Rabin, "Testimony," 147–65.

The maneuvers of Ordlaf and the timely intervention of Alfred hardly reflect the portrait of impartial royal justice emphasized by Asser in the final chapter of his biography of the king.[141] The dismissive references to Æthelm Higa's suit and the circumvention of local authority to seek royal favor appear to undermine the decrees in royal legislation that every person was entitled to the benefit of law, regardless of station. Moreover, the relatively lenient treatment of Helmstan for his thefts – even when caught in the act – bears little resemblance to the harsh punishments meted out to thieves under the laws of Alfred and his successors. Yet while a modern reader might be forgiven for viewing the Fonthill Letter as an unapologetic record of legal corruption, there is little reason to think that it was seen as such when it was composed. Ordlaf makes no effort to conceal his peddling of influence. Indeed, he depicts his support of Helmstan as the proper action of a godfather towards his godson and bases his appeal to Edward the Elder on the assertion that the son should not overturn his father's judgment. Likewise, although the loss of property and legal status left Helmstan a bankrupt tenant on his godfather's lands, he never suffered the branding, loss of limb, or execution suffered by less fortunate miscreants such as the widow accused of witchcraft, discussed in section 3.

The complexities of the Fonthill Letter highlight the difficulties involved in understanding how law was enforced and the means by which wrongdoers were penalized. Although the exhaustive injury schedules and apparently comprehensive list of misdeeds found in royal legislation suggest a legal community – both local and kingdomwide – fully prepared to rectify violations of the peace, the translation from text to practice was by no means a smooth one. The absence of any sort of large-scale enforcement apparatus, the traditional practice of private redress in cases of personal injury, and the tension between regional, ecclesiastical, and royal authority all combined to produce a complex web of jurisdictions and widely differing views of what it meant to enforce the law.

4.1 Investigation and Apprehension

Among the more unusual aspects of the Fonthill Letter is its detailed account of the manner in which Helmstan's crimes were investigated and the means by which he was identified as the culprit. Wulfstan's abortive attempt at cattle theft failed when "his speremon ahredde ða sporwreclas. Ða he fleah ða torypte hine an breber ofer ðæt nebb. Ða ætsacan wolde, ða sæde him mon ðæt to tacne" (the tracker recovered the traced cattle. When he [Helmstan] fled, a bramble scratched his face. Then, when he wished to deny [his crime], that was declared

---

[141] Asser, *Vita Alfredi*, ch. 106, ed. in Stevenson, *Asser's Life*, 92–96.

a sign of his guilt).[142] Several features of this account stand out: first, the term *speremon* indicates that the references in the laws of Edward and Æthelstan to a class of persons specifically tasked with the tracing of lost cattle were likely grounded in actual practice;[143] second, both the tracking of the cattle and the subsequent tracking of Helmstan himself indicate that some degree of investigation was required both to recover the stolen animals and to identify the culprit; and third, that the presence of physical evidence in the form of the facial scratches was deemed sufficiently convincing to negate any exculpatory oaths that may have been offered by Helmstan's supporters. The cumulative effect is an impression of a sophisticated apparatus for the recovery of stolen property and the arrest and prosecution of the culprit.

Yet the sorry conclusion to Helmstan's abortive career as a cattle rustler may not be typical of pre-Conquest law enforcement. The *speremon* who pursued Helmstan was most likely a servant of the herd's owner, whose wealth afforded him resources unavailable to those of lower status. In the majority of cases, the absence of a state-supported law enforcement apparatus meant that responsibility for the investigation and prosecution of offenses lay with the injured party. Although penalties for the violation of royal or ecclesiastical prerogatives were assessed by the representatives of king or church, for the most part legal remedies for theft, personal injury (including manslaughter), dishonest trade practices, and other similar misdeeds could be pursued only after the swearing of a formal oath of accusation against the presumed culprit by the victim or his family. In the absence of evidence, however, it is difficult to know what sorts of investigations took place prior to such oaths or even how many offenses required an investigatory process to identify the culprit. One might even question the percentage of disputes that ended up in court at all, as many – perhaps the majority – were doubtless resolved through arbitration, compromise, or other forms of private action.

One tantalizing category of evidence for the ways in which individuals sought remedies for theft or injury survives in the form of charms and quasi-religious rituals intended to recover stolen goods and identify those responsible for theft or injury. Typical is the ritual transcribed in the twelfth-century legal anthology *Textus Roffensis* which requires its incantation to be sung "on feower healfa þæs huses and æne on middan" (on the four sides of the house and once in the middle). The incantation itself reads,

Crux Christi reducat. Crux Christi per furtum periit, inventa est.
Abraham tibi semitas, vias, montes concludat, Job et flumina.
Ad iudicium ligatum perducat.

---

[142] Hough, "Cattle-Tracking," 864–92. [143] *II Edward* 4 and *II Æthelstan* 2.

Judeas xri Crist ahengon, ðæt him com to wite swa strangum.

Gedydon heom dæda þa wyrstan, hi þæt drofe forguldon.

Hælon hit him to hearme miclum, and heo hit na forhelan ne mihton.

May Christ's Cross return it. Christ's Cross which was lost through theft is found.

May Abraham close to you the paths, the ways, [and] the mountains, and Job the
streams.

May [you] be brought bound to judgment.

The Jews hanged Christ, for which a great punishment came to them.

They committed the worst of acts towards him, they paid terribly for that.

They hid it to their own great harm, and they could not keep it hidden.[144]

Perhaps the most striking features of texts of this sort are the circumstances of
their preservation. The cattle-theft rite survives in *Textus Roffensis* alongside
more traditional legal texts without explicit markers indicating a difference in
genre or usage. Comparison with earlier versions from other manuscripts
reveals that the meter of the *Textus* incantation has been regularized and the
references to Abraham and Job reworked to more accurately reflect their
biblical source. The care taken in revising the *Textus* ritual as well as its survival
in a high-status manuscript suggests that we would be wrong to dismiss it as
either a superstitious practice of the poorly educated or as evidence of an
irrational strain in pre-Conquest legal thought ultimately superseded by more
modern practices of criminal investigation. Rather, such rituals were seen as
part of the investigatory process and viewed as no less rational than the
employment of a *speremon* to track lost cattle. Put differently, in the pursuit
of wrongdoers, the trained eye of the tracker was no less important than the all-
seeing eye of God.

4.2 The Trial

Once the perpetrator was identified, the community's response could range from
extra-legal violence to a formal trial and punishment before a local court. The ease
with which feelings of grievance could turn into a desire for revenge made the
period before the trial a dangerous one for the accused, for whom the safest option
was often to claim sanctuary.[145] The peace and protection of the church was
guaranteed by the first statute of the laws of Æthelbert (though this clause was
likely added to the text after its initial promulgation) and remained a consistent
feature of royal legislation until the Conquest. The laws of Ine, for instance, exempt
a fugitive from the death penalty if he manages to flee to a church and claim

---

[144] Text edited in Hollis, "Cattle-Theft Charms," 146–49. For further discussion, see Rabin, "Ritual
Magic," 177–96 and Cooper, "Episcopal Power," 193–214.

[145] See section 3.1.3.

ecclesiastical protection. Alfred expands on Ine's provision in two significant ways: First, he guarantees the fugitive three days of absolute sanctuary if he reaches any ecclesiastical property, not just a church; second, he grants that the protected fugitive's free confession to any hitherto unknown crimes will diminish any penalty he might have faced by half.[146] The laws composed by Archbishop Wulfstan echo a theme common in his political tracts and homilies, namely, that the protection of the church is superior even to that of the king, yet both were nonetheless equally inviolable. Moreover, it was among the king's principal duties to ensure that neither he nor his subordinates impinged upon the church's preroga-tive. By this time, the boundaries of ecclesiastical sanctuary had expanded such that it encompassed lands as much as one mile in every direction from the church's door.[147] Although the degree of sanctuary an individual church was able to grant depended in part upon its status, violating the protection of even the smallest church was no less serious than violating that of a cathedral.[148] A narrative from the reign of Æthelred indicates the seriousness with which sanctuary protections were held: as punishment for attempting to defy the sanctuary of the abbey of Bury St. Edmunds, a corrupt reeve was possessed by a demon and driven mad until he died. Unable to rest quietly in the grave, however, his corpse haunted the town, which could only be rid of him by sewing the corpse into a calf's skin and sinking it to the bottom of a local lake.[149] Much like other early medieval narratives of the unquiet dead, the presence of an ambulatory corpse implies not only that the reeve himself was guilty of a violation against the church but that the town itself was tainted by his sin and so also in need of expiation.

On its face, the dispute between reeve and church in the St. Edmunds *miraculum* illustrates the conflict between the flawed law of the world and the perfect law of heaven. In so doing, it dramatizes the ever-present tension between secular and sacred authority. Yet it also highlights another issue of equal importance to the exercise of early English law, namely, the question of which court held jurisdiction in any particular dispute. The legal landscape of pre-Conquest England was a patchwork of competing authorities – royal, aristocratic, local, and ecclesiastical – each seeking to gain priority over its fellows. The resulting confusion was such that one historian has observed that "in the minds of malefactors there must have been considerable uncertainty as to who would have the privilege of indicting or hanging them."[150] Disputes over

---

[146] *Ine* 5 and *Alfred* 2.1, 5.4, and 42.2.   [147] Shoemaker, *Sanctuary and Crime*, 110.

[148] *VIII Æthelred* 5–5.1. See also section 3.1.3.

[149] Archdeacon Herman, *De miraculis sancti Edmundi*, ch. 3, ed. in License, *Herman the Archdeacon*, 10–15.

[150] Putnam, "Transformation," 21. Similar observations have been made more recently in Wormald, "Lordship and Justice," 332, and Hudson, *Oxford History*, 64–65.

jurisdiction are a common feature of pre-Conquest legal records. For instance, it is Leofwine's challenge to Æthelred's jurisdiction that forces the king to remand his dispute with Wynflæd to a lower court. Likewise, in the Fonthill Letter, the failure of Æthelm Higa's suit proceeds from Ordlaf's success in convincing Alfred to assign the dispute to a court presided over by Ordlaf himself. While these disputes primarily concern questions of property ownership, the stakes in claiming jurisdiction in a criminal prosecution could be much higher. In another (this time post-Conquest) dispute from Bury St. Edmunds, Jocelin of Brakelond records that the town leaders challenged the abbot and chapter over the fate of an alleged thief. Although the man lived in town, jurisdiction over his property was held by the church, which compelled him to engage in trial by combat and, when he lost, sentenced him to death. However, had he lived just a street or two over, he would have been subject to secular authority, and rather than being forced into ritual combat, he would have had the opportunity to exonerate himself by the oaths of his neighbors.[151] Given cases like this, it can hardly be surprising that disputants, plaintiffs, and defendants would go to great lengths – even, as in the case of Ordlaf, petitioning the king himself – to ensure that their case would be heard by a sympathetic court.

The court itself, whether civil or ecclesiastical, would be overseen by a panel of judges that included *ealdormen*, influential local landowners, high-ranking members of the church, and perhaps a representative of the king. The earliest reference to such a panel occurs in the laws of Hlothhere and Eadric, which grant the "deman Cantwara" (judges of the Kentish people) the right to adjudicate disputes.[152] Roughly two centuries later, Asser describes Alfred's personal interest in the rulings of his justices and his review of judgments to ensure none were influenced by "amore vel timore aut aliorum odio aut etiam pro alicuius pecuniae cubiditate" (love or fear of anyone, or hatred of others; or also for the desire of money).[153]

We would do well not to take Asser at his word: the lack of bias he claims Alfred prioritized so highly does not entirely agree with the depiction of judicial activity in other texts. In the Fonthill Letter, Ordlaf himself sits on the judicial panel that exonerates Helmstan and permits him to regain his property (at least, initially). It must be emphasized, though, that shady as such transactions might appear today, there is little reason to believe that they were thought so at the time. Ordlaf freely admits his participation in the judicial panel without any indication of shame or concern that his involvement might be perceived as wrongdoing. Indeed, it appears to have been seen as normal – especially in

---

[151] See Butler, *The Chronicle of Jocelin*, 100–101.   [152] *Hlothhere and Eadric* 8.
[153] Asser, *Vita Alfredi*, ch. 106, ed. Stevenson, *Asser's Life*, 93.

small communities – for local dignitaries to sit in judgment over disputes involving their kin.[154] The fact that this was the case points to a crucial aspect of early English dispute resolution, one that has been touched on before: the purpose of a courtroom proceeding was less to enact perfect justice than it was to restore harmony within the community. Put differently, the goal of the judicial panel was less a literal-minded enforcement of the law than a negotiation intended to ensure that communal bonds – though stretched – would not be broken; for otherwise, in the words of the Wynflæd-Leofwine charter, "nar freondscype nære" (there would be no friendship).

The rules of procedure by which a pre-Conquest court functioned remain somewhat amorphous. Procedural statutes in Old English royal legislation suggest that courts relied primarily on oath-helpers; that is, those willing to swear to the integrity of the litigant, defendant, or plaintiff. The number of oath-helpers required followed a strict calculus determined by an individual's status and character. Those unable to produce the required number of supporters or with a reputation for wrongful behavior were deemed not "aþ-wyrþe" (oath-worthy) and thus without the means to defend themselves or their property in court. However, there is little external evidence to suggest that courts actually functioned with this degree of rigid formality. A different picture of early English evidentiary procedure can be found in an Old English oath formulary *Swerian*, which includes oaths for a range of persons and situations, including the taking of evidence and testimony in a manner resembling that of a modern court. Indeed, one of the distinguishing features of pre-Conquest law was the importance it placed on direct testimony – that which witnesses "eagum ofer-seah 7 earum oferhyrdon" (saw with their eyes and heard with their ears) – relative to its continental counterparts.[155] One charter lists three forms of evidentiary testimony "wyrðe ðe eallum leodscipe geseald" (officially permitted to all people): assertion of claim (*tale*), vouching to warranty (*team*), and the oath of ownership (*ahnung*).[156] Also suggestive is the absence of direct references to royal legislation in surviving dispute records, indicating that although the king's laws may have provided a framework within which cases were resolved, the primary factors in adjudication remained the particulars of the situation and the customs of the community.[157] In other words, dispute resolution was guided as much by communal norms as it was by legal rules. These

---

[154] This phenomenon has been observed in later English law as well. See Johnson, *Law in Common*, 19–54.

[155] *Swerian* 8. On this point, see Harmer, *Writs*, 535; Wormald, *Making*, 384; Kelly, "Written Word," 50–51; Rabin, "Testimony," and "Witnessing Kingship," 220 n. 4. Regarding the distinction between Old English testimony practices and those described in the Salic Law, see Drew, *Salian Franks*, 38–39.

[156] S 1457.   [157] See section 4.3.

norms reflected a combination of legal, social, and religious factors – implicitly agreed upon though largely unwritten – which were the criteria according to which disputes were judged.[158] It would be wrong to take this argument too far: Old English legal practice was far more than simply an exercise in situational ethics and some dispute records do depict courts conforming to royal law even if the law itself was not explicitly cited. Nonetheless, when Æthelred commissioned the judges in the dispute between Wynflæd and Leofwine to settle things in a way "that seemed most just to them," the king's commission entailed, at least in part, a recognition that the particular norms underlying the suit and its context demanded a resolution that reflected those norms.

Viewing early English court procedure as an expression of social norms helps explain the role of the ordeal, which remains for many historians one of the most puzzling aspects of medieval law. Reliance upon the *iudicium Dei* (judgment of God) took many forms in pre-Conquest England, including trial by combat, trial by hot iron or fire, trial by water, and trial by *corsnæd* (in which the accused must swallow a morsel of stale bread without choking).[159] Although clauses related to the ordeal are a common feature of royal legislation, there is little evidence to suggest that the practice was as widespread as the laws suggest. Courts appear to have resorted to the ordeal most often when the accused, as a stranger or otherwise without family or friends, lacked a local support network to validate his oath. In effect, the ordeal was a ritual designed to enlist the testimony of God when earthly witnesses were wanting. This is not to suggest that ordeals were viewed uncritically by either lawmakers or laypeople. Indeed, the ordeal's shortcomings and its susceptibility to abuse were well-known to early medieval authors: in the tenth-century *Translatio et miracula Sancti Swithuni* (translation and miracles of Saint Swithun) by the monk Lantfred, for instance, a corrupt reeve, "*ultramodum superbiens pro mundanis facibus*" (exulting overmuch in his worldly authority), increased both the weight and heat of the iron used in an ordeal in order to ensure that the accused would be found guilty.[160] Yet ordeals were not merely a means of ascertaining guilt; rather, they were public spectacles designed to integrate legal and religious rituals in order to validate the authority of the law. Clauses concerning ordeals

---

[158] Hyams, "Norms and Legal Argument," 41–61 and Hudson, "Court Cases and Legal Arguments," 91–93.

[159] There are many excellent studies on the medieval ordeal, the most immediately relevant of which are Bartlett, *Trial by Fire and Water*; Hyams, "Trial by Ordeal," 90–126; Keefer, "The *Corsnæd* Ordeal," 237–64; Keefer, "The Anglo-Saxon Lay Ordeal," 353–68; Niles, "Trial By Ordeal," 369–82; Hudson, *Oxford History*, 84–87; and Whitman, *The Origins of Reasonable Doubt*, 50–90.

[160] Lantfred, *Translatio et miracula Sancti Swithuni*, cap. 25, ed. in Lapidge, *The Cult of St Swithun*, 308–11.

describe their procedures with far greater detail than those dealing with oath-helping or other ritualized legal practices. The tenth-century tract *Ordal*, for instance, specifies how far a proband must carry a hot iron, how the heat of the iron was to be tested, the witnesses necessary to validate the proceeding, and the place where they should stand in relation to the accused. It also required those present – accused, judges, and spectators alike – to have fasted, abstained from sexual activity, tasted and been sprinkled with holy water, and kissed both the cross and the Bible.[161] This emphasis on performance suggests that the spectacle of the ordeal was directed as much at the ritual's witnesses as it was at the court or accused. Insofar as the ordeal invites the divine to intervene in the workings of human justice, the detailed strictures concerning how the ordeal may be not just undergone but *seen*, marks the community as its subject no less than the accused. Accordingly, relying upon divine intervention in worldly justice served as a means of rendering the foreign, marginalized or unknown knowable, thereby subordinating the alien to the norms of the community.

4.3 The Sentence

The guilt of the accused having been established, the judicial panel had a wide range of penalties at its disposal. In the Kentish laws of the seventh century, the principle underlying the sentencing of the accused reflected what in modern terms is referred to as restorative justice. That is, in sentencing the offender, the court sought to compensate the victim to fully make up for what had been lost. A guide to appropriate compensation could be found in the lengthy injury schedule that takes up the majority of the laws of Æthelberht. The advantages to such a system were threefold: First, compensatory payments by the perpetrator to the victim provided a substitute for extra-legal violence in the form of vengeance or feud; second, in regularizing penalties across the kingdom, it discouraged would-be miscreants from breaking the law in one area rather than another in order to ensure a lighter sentence; and third, it established the king's authority to claim for himself the prerogative to determine the seriousness of a crime and the appropriate means by which the victim may be compensated.

The consistency with which financial compensation was used as a penalty, both in the laws of kings of Kent and those issued by later rulers, provides valuable evidence for the evolving definition of legal violation. The most important feature of this evolution is a changing notion of what is being violated when a law is broken. In other words, the restorative model employed by Æthelberht treated the wrongful act as primarily an injury to an individual, and so the individual was the rightful recipient of compensation. Later

---

[161] *Ordal*, 1–6.

legislation, however, distributed the proceeds from financial penalties differently. In cases of theft or personal injury, for instance, a fine (sometimes totaling
the entirety of the thief's property) was to be paid to the king in addition to any
compensation offered the victim.[162] The implication is that the culprit not only
harmed an individual, but also violated the king's *mund*, that is, his authority
and protection. Penalties increased if the offense was committed on the king's
property or, more seriously, in the presence of the king himself. A similar
approach to the assessment of compensation can also be found in the clauses
concerning other forms of wrongdoing. Thus, failure to pay dues owed to the
church demanded that the delinquent pay compensation to the bishop as injured
party and to the king, whose protection of the church has been violated.
Likewise, injuries to a slave or a tenant farmer required the payment of
compensation to the property owner who would be deprived of the injured
subordinate's labor.[163] However, perhaps the most revealing distribution of
compensation is that involving sexual offenses: under the laws of Alfred,
compensation for rape or sexual assault is paid directly to the injured woman.
In contrast, the laws of Æthelred and Cnut decree that penalties should instead
be paid to the woman's male guardian or, if one is lacking, to the king. The
distribution of compensation thereby charts two developments in early English
law: First, it reflects an increasingly broad understanding of royal authority
according to which any violation of the king's law – even if the king is not
directly the injured party – is an offense against the king himself; and second,
the right to compensation becomes a means of distinguishing between fully
entitled subjects of the law and those who – for reasons of gender, age, or
financial status – are considered more marginal figures whose identity is defined
primarily by their dependence upon a guardian or patron.

In certain cases, however, the payment of compensation was deemed an
inadequate means of addressing the offender's actions. Either because of the
seriousness of the crime or the poverty of the culprit, other measures were
needed to penalize the guilty and satisfy the community's sense of justice. In
some cases, those lacking financial resources may have faced some form of
imprisonment, though this is mentioned only very rarely in the documentary
record. More frequently, the courts resorted to legal enslavement or, if an
individual was already a slave, public whipping. The laws make several references to "witeþeowan" (penal slaves), those reduced to slavery either tempor-
arily or permanently because of their misdeeds. Slavery was a common practice
in early medieval England and, though the enslaved did have some protections,
for the most part the slave was wholly subject to the demands of their owner.

---

[162] *II Cnut* 30.9.   [163] *IV Æthelstan* 6.6.

Although some slight evidence suggests that *nydþeowan*, those enslaved because of debt, may have been treated at least a little more favorably; those enslaved for wrongdoing could expect much more severe treatment, including unregulated labor and physical abuse.[164]

The second circumstance in which compensation was considered inadequate was as a penalty for a class of crimes known as *botleas*: acts so serious that no amends (*bot*), however great, could make up for the harm caused by the perpetrator. Violations deemed *botleas* included housebreaking, arson, theft, murder (especially if committed in a church), and treachery. Other misdeeds, such as perjury or the violation of royal protection, are not explicitly referred to as *botleas* but were treated with similar severity. Lesser penalties for acts of this sort included branding or amputation, while those guilty of more serious crimes would be sentenced to death. Punishments of this kind were not intended merely to cause additional pain to the guilty or set a greater example for the innocent; rather, the penalty was designed to permanently mark the malefactor's body in a way that reflected the nature of their crime. Perjurers, for instance, might lose the hand with which they swore the false oath. Likewise, a woman guilty of adultery would be condemned to lose her nose and both of her ears, presumably to deprive her of the physical beauty that tempted her and her lover into sin.[165] Among the most significant consequences of such penalties was their permanence: the wound would forever mark the criminal with their crime. Indeed, given the grotesque results of punishments of this type, the identity of the offender would come to be defined by the act that led to their visual disfigurement. To witness their punishment – not just in the moment it took place but as a permanent presence in their lives – was to witness also the violence visited upon those who flout legal authority.[166] The guilty thus became living symbols of the law's authority.

For the most serious crimes – particularly theft, treachery, housebreaking, and homicide – the penalty was death. However, despite modern assumptions, putting an offender to death was far more controversial than one might expect. Although surviving dispute records suggest that early medieval England was not lacking in persons willing to break the law with both enthusiasm and creativity, only a very few records indicate that such individuals were put to death for their crimes. The evidence of royal legislation is ambiguous: in the thirty-eight pre-Conquest law codes attributed to specific kings, references to the death penalty occur in just seventy-eight clauses, the earliest of which appear in the seventh-century West Saxon laws of Ine and Kentish laws of Wihtred, and the latest in the eleventh-century laws of Cnut. However, even this

---

[164] Pelteret, *Slavery*, 80–108.   [165] *II Cnut* 53.   [166] O'Keeffe, "Body and Law," 217–18.

number over-represents the frequency of capital penalties, since a disproportionate number of these clauses – twenty-eight, or approximately 36 percent of the total – occur in the laws promulgated by Æthelstan. Taken as a whole, however, death penalty clauses fall into three categories. The smallest, containing fifteen clauses (approximately 19 percent of the total), treat capital punishment simply as a condition for further action, as in *Wihtred* 22.1: "Gif hine man acwelle, þam agende hine man healfne agelde" (If [a slave] is executed, his master shall be paid half his value). Those in the second category, containing twenty-seven clauses (approximately 34 percent), reserve the death penalty as a possible sentence for criminal activity; however, other potential actions – including a lesser punishment or royal pardon – are listed also. For instance, *Ine* 6 decrees: "Gif hwa gefeohte on cyninges huse, sie he scyldig ealles his ierfes, 7 sie on cyninges dome hwæðer he lif age þe nage" (If anyone fights in the house of the king, he shall forfeit all that he owns and it will be according to the king's judgment whether he lives or not). In the final category, containing thirty-seven clauses (approximately 47 percent of the total), are those clauses in which the death penalty is ruled to be the sole appropriate punishment for criminal activity. Grouped in this way, the distribution of clauses seems to suggest a fairly robust royal enthusiasm for putting lawbreakers to death, yet here again the numbers are skewed by the rather draconian laws of Æthelstan. If these are omitted, a very different picture emerges: of the fifty remaining clauses, only twenty (40 percent) prescribe death as a mandatory sentence; in contrast, the majority of the clauses – twenty-five (50 percent) – now list the death penalty as only one among several possible juridical responses to a criminal action.[167] Viewed from this perspective, clauses concerning capital punishment appear to serve much the same purpose as those, discussed above, regulating monetary compensation: that is, they functioned less as legal dicta commanding strict obedience than as political statements designed to establish a particular royal prerogative. Indeed, they often seem less concerned with actually executing offenders than with reserving the king's right to do so. In this way, they advance a claim regarding the extent of royal power while also recognizing the political challenges that would arise should that claim be asserted too aggressively.

Indications of what challenges of this sort might look like are not difficult to find. The frustration of kings such as Edward the Martyr, Æthelred, and Edward the Confessor when faced with a stubborn – and at times rebellious – aristocracy provides a vivid reminder of the sorts of political barriers checking the spread of royal power. No less important were the church's longstanding concerns over

---

[167] These statistics are taken from Rabin, "Capital Punishment," 185–86.

the morality of capital punishment. The potential for error or bias sparked ecclesiastical fears of violating the divine precept in *Deuteronomy* 32:35: "Mea est ultio, et ego retribuam" (Vengeance is mine and I will repay). The *Old English Boethius*, for instance, cautions that, "ælc unriht witnung sie [þæs] yfel þe hit doð, næs þas ðe hit þafað, forþam his yfel hine gedeð earmne" (each unjust punishment is an evil for the one who inflicts it, not the one who endures it, because his evil makes him miserable).[168] Likewise, Ælfric of Eynsham cautioned Archbishop Wulfstan in a letter, "We ne moton beon ymbe mannes deaðe. Þeah he manslaga beo oþþe morð gefremede oþþe mycel þeofman, swa-þeah we ne scylan him dead getæcean" (We must not be implicated in a man's death. Even if he has committed manslaughter or murder or he is a great thief, nonetheless we must not pronounce death for him).[169] That these were more than empty platitudes is suggested by an addendum to *VI Æthelstan* in which the king, addressing Archbishop Wulfhelm of Canterbury, agreed to raise the minimum age for execution from twelve to fifteen.[170] Stronger steps were taken by Wulfstan, who lessened the number of crimes punishable by execution and proclaimed in *II Cnut* that (we forbeodað þæt man Cristene men for ealles to lytlum huru to deaþe ne forræde; ac elles geræde man friðlice steora folce to þearfe and ne forspille for lytlum Godes handgeweorc and his agenne ceap, þe he deore gebohte" (we forbid Christians to be sentenced to death for entirely too little; instead, merciful penalties are to be established for the good of the people, and so that God's handiwork, which he paid for himself at a high cost, not be destroyed because of petty crimes).[171] To aggressively assert a claim that the king held absolute judicial power with the right to define at whim those acts deserving of execution thus carried with it the threat of resistance from both church and aristocracy. Although executions were undoubtedly carried out and mercy at times certainly granted, the authority under which such decisions were made remained very much in dispute.

Taken together, the various means by which those who violated the law were investigated, tried, and sentenced suggests an essentially pragmatic view of legal practice. Although diverse sets of rules, regulations, norms, and precepts governed the various stages of prosecution, there was sufficient flexibility within these strictures to account for the peculiarities of individual cases, the distinct customs and practices of particular regions, and the specific aims and ideologies of different political institutions. The ambiguity of Æthelred's

---

[168] Godden and Irvine, *Boethius,* chap. 38, lines 225–26, vol. I, p. 357. On this passage, see Marafioti, "Earthly Justice," 120–21.

[169] Ælfric, *Second Old English Letter to Wulfstan*, ed. Fehr, *Die Hirtenbriefe Ælfrics*, 140. On this passage, see Marafioti, "Punishing Bodies and Saving Souls," 44–45.

[170] *VI Æthelstan* 12.1.   [171] *II Cnut* 2.1.

command that the judges in the dispute between Wynflæd and Leofwine act in the manner that seemed most just to them can thus be understood as an expression of the necessary elasticity underlying pre-Conquest legal culture. Within this context, *riht* was not necessarily a matter of decree but of negotiation.

5 Conclusion: Thinking Law

This book began by asking how Æthelred might have been understood when he ordered the dispute between Wynflæd and Leofwine to be resolved in the "rihtlicost" (most just) fashion. Was his understanding of the meaning of *rihtlicost* shared by others party to the dispute – judges, witnesses, and litigants? And in a broader sense, how were different – often competing – interpretations of a concept like *riht* influenced by factors such as status, gender, royal imperative, and local norms? The answer to these questions is not a simple one. Although those of different status or community were eager to characterize their own version of *riht* as "most just," all too frequently proponents of one view found themselves in conflict with proponents of another. Within this context, the idea of *riht* might thus be better understood, not as static or universal, but as an evolving concept always in the process of being reshaped by conflict, negotiation, and compromise.

Understanding pre-Conquest legal culture in this way highlights one of its foundational – if often overlooked – principles: that the law was not merely a list of rules to be observed but a set of values to be internalized. A passage such as Wulfstan's call in *II Cnut* for each loyal reader to "inweardre heortan gebuga-[n]" (submit in his innermost heart) was designed to impress upon its audience that adherence to the law was more than just a matter of behavior. Rather, obedience to the laws of king and church was a primary structural component of an individual's identity as a faithful legal subject.[172] Wulfstan expands on this theme with his use of the three-orders trope. The trope enables him to conceptualize an ideal Christian society which defines each order by its obligation to the whole (to fight, work, or pray) while also imposing upon its individual members an ethical demand to conform in behavior and morals to the order in which God has placed them. A similar imperative can be found in the charter recording the accusation of witchcraft against the Ailsworth widow. In emphasizing the royal sanction for the accusers' unorthodox actions, the text requires that the reader, despite any misgivings, either accept the king's judgment as a faithful subject or be grouped with the witch and her outlaw son, unfaithful to both God and king. The rhetorical structure of the Fonthill Letter works in much

---

[172] On this point, see Musson, *Medieval Law in Context,* 1–2.

the same way: as Ordlaf reminds Alfred's son Edward, royal authority rests in large part on continuity from one reign to the next, for "gif mon ælcne dom wile onwendan ðe Ælfred cing gesette hwonne habbe we ðonne gemotad?" (if one wishes to change every judgment which King Alfred gave, when will we ever finish disputing?). In short, for a judgment to be truly just it must withstand the change in ruler. To reject Alfred's judgment – whether as king or subject – is to reject the legal authority upon which it was based, an act of bad faith that threatens the continuity of government and the stability of the kingdom itself. Within this context, Æthelred's command that the dispute be resolved in the most just fashion involves more than just the determination of a fair and lawful ruling. It also grounds any ruling by the judges or settlement by the litigants in their knowledge of the law and fidelity to the king. At issue was not just the settlement deemed *rihtlicost*, but also the processes of thought by which the most just resolution had been reached – how, in other words, justice *seemed* (geseman) to them. As the participants in the dispute recognized, pre-Conquest law was a matter of mind as well as act.

The study of early medieval notions of crime and punishment, law and lawlessness, dispute and settlement thus encompasses more than just documentary or political history. It is also a history of the ways in which law was made, received, understood, enforced, and internalized. For the privileged, the law afforded them the agency necessary to fulfill their aspirations for themselves, their kindred, and their community. For the less privileged, the law defined the boundaries of acceptable behavior and set the limits within (and against) which they could pursue goals of their own. In each case, however, the law functioned as the framework by which its subjects came to be defined within the political world of pre-Conquest England. The resources, strategies, and arguments that Wynflæd and Leofwine brought to bear upon their dispute indicate more than just their social connections or the types of legal activity available to them. They also reveal something of their different experiences of law and the ways in which those experiences shaped their relationship to the king, the court, the disputed land, and each other. For Wynflæd, Leofwine, and their contemporaries, the law not only set the rules by which the realm was governed but, more importantly, it served as an arena within which its subjects could dispute, compromise, argue, and negotiate, all to determine what truly seemed most just to them.

Bibliography

Primary Sources

Attenborough, F. L. (1922) *The Laws of the Earliest English Kings*. Cambridge: Cambridge University Press.

Brooks, Nicholas, and S. E. Kelly. (2013) *Charters of Christ Church, Canterbury*. Anglo-Saxon Charters 17. 2 vols. Oxford: Oxford University Press.

Butler, H. E. (1949) *The Chronicle of Jocelin of Brakelond*. Nelson's Medieval Classics. London: Thomas Nelson and Sons, Ltd.

Campbell, Alistair. (1973) *Charters of Rochester*. Anglo-Saxon Charters 1. Oxford: Oxford University Press.

Colgrave, Bertram, and R. A. B. Mynors. (1991) *Bede's Ecclesiastical History of the English People*. Oxford: Clarendon Press.

Drew, Katherine Fischer. (1991) *The Laws of the Salian Franks*. Philadelphia: University of Pennsylvania Press.

Fehr, Bernard. (1914) *Die Hirtenbriefe Ælfrics in altenglischer und lateinischer Fassung*. Bibliothek der angelsächsischen Prosa. Hamburg: H. Grand.

Harmer, Florence E. (1952) *Anglo-Saxon Writs*. Manchester: Manchester University Press.

Jenkins, Dafydd. (1990) *Hywel Dda: The Law*. Carmarthen: Gomer Press.

Jost, Karl. (1959) *Die "Institutes of Polity, Civil and Ecclesiastical"*. Bern: Francke Verlag.

Kelly, S. E. (2009) *Charters of Peterborough Abbey*. Anglo-Saxon Charters 14. Oxford: Oxford University Press.

Lapidge, Michael. (2003) *The Cult of St Swithun*. Winchester Studies 4. Oxford: Oxford University Press.

Licence, Tom. (2014) *Herman the Archdeacon and Goscelin of Saint-Bertin: Miracles of St. Edmund*. Oxford Medieval Texts. Oxford: Oxford University Press.

Liebermann, Felix. (1903–1916) *Die Gesetze Der Angelsachsen*. 3 vols. Halle: Scientia Aalen.

Miller, Sean. (2001) *Charters of New Minster, Winchester*. Anglo-Saxon Charters 9. Oxford: Oxford University Press.

Napier, Arthur. (1883) *Wulfstan: Sammlung der ihm zugeschreiben homilien nebst Untersuchungen über ihre Echteit*. Berlin: Weidmannsche Buchhandlung.

O'Donovan, M. A. (1988) *Charters of Sherborne*. Vol. 3 of Anglo-Saxon Charters. Oxford: Oxford University Press.

Oliver, Lisi. (2002) *The Beginnings of English Law.* Toronto: University of Toronto Press.

Rabin, Andrew. (2015) *The Political Writings of Archbishop Wulfstan of York.* Manchester: Manchester University Press.

Robertson, A. J. (1925) *The Laws of the Kings of England from Edmund to Henry I.* Cambridge: Cambridge University Press.

(1956) *Anglo-Saxon Charters.* 2nd ed. Cambridge: Cambridge University Press.

Stevenson, William Henry. (1959) *Asser's Life of King Alfred, Together with the Annals of Saint Neots Erroneously Ascribed to Asser.* Oxford: Clarendon Press.

Symons, Dom Thomas. (1953) *Regularis Concordia Anglicae Nationis Monachorum Sanctimonialiumque* (*the Monastic Agreement of the Monks and Nuns of the English Nation*). London: Thomas Nelson and Sons Ltd.

Whitelock, Dorothy. (1930) *Anglo-Saxon Wills.* Cambridge Studies in English Legal History. Cambridge: University Press.

(1981) *Councils and Synods with Other Documents Relating to the English Church: 871–1066.* Vol. I, part 1. Oxford: Clarendon Press.

Williams, Ann and G. H. Martin. (1992) *Domesday Book.* New York: Penguin Books.

Secondary Sources

Abels, Richard. (1988) *Lordship and Military Obligation in Anglo-Saxon England.* London: British Museum Publications.

Ammon, Matthias. (2013) '*Ge mid wedde ge mid aðe*': The Functions of Oath and Pledge in Anglo-Saxon Legal Culture. *Historical Research* 86(233): 515–35.

Bartlett, Robert. (1986) *Trial by Fire and Water: The Medieval Judicial Ordeal.* Oxford: Clarendon Press.

Baxter, Stephen. (2009) The Limits of the Late Anglo-Saxon State. In Walter Pohl and Veronika Wieser, eds., *Der Frühmittelalterliche Staat: Europäische Perspektiven. Forschungen Zur Geschichte Des Mittelalters.* Vienna: Österreichische Akademie der Wissenschaften: 503–15.

Bremmer, Rolf H., Jr. (2019) Proverbs in the Anglo-Saxon Laws. In Stefan Jurasinski and Andrew Rabin, eds., *Languages of the Law in Early Medieval England: Essays in Memory of Lisi Oliver.* Vol. 22 of Mediaevalia Groningana New Series. Leuven: Peeters: 179–92.

Brooks, Nicholas P. (2009) The Fonthill Letter, Ealdorman Ordlaf, and Anglo-Saxon Law in Practice. In Stephen Baxter, Catherine E. Karkov,

Janet Nelson, and David Pelteret, eds., *Early Medieval Studies in Memory of Patrick Wormald*. Aldershot: Ashgate: 301–18.

(2015) The Laws of Æthelberht of Kent: Preservation, Content, and Composition. In Bruce O'Brien and Barbara Bombi, eds., *Textus Roffensis: Law, Language, and Libraries in Early Medieval England*. Turnhout: Brepols: 105–36.

Brown, Warren. (2002) Charters as Weapons: On the Role Played by Early Medieval Dispute Records in the Disputes They Record. *Journal of Medieval History* 28(3): 227–48.

Campbell, James. (2000) The Late Anglo-Saxon State: A Maximum View. In James Campbell, ed., *The Anglo-Saxon State*. New York: Hambledon: 1–30.

Carella, Bryan. (2015) Asser's Bible and the Prologue to the Laws of Alfred. *Anglia* 130(2): 195–206.

(2015) The Earliest Expression for Outlawry in Anglo-Saxon Law. *Traditio* 70: 111–43.

Chaplais, Pierre. (1969) Who Introduced Charters into England? The Case for Augustine. *Journal of the Society of Archivists* 3(10): 526–42.

Coleman, Julie. (1998) Rape in Anglo-Saxon England. In Guy Halsall, ed. *Violence and Society in the Early Medieval West*. Woodbridge: Boydell: 193–204.

Cooper, Tracey-Anne. (2015) Episcopal Power and Performance: The Fugitive Thief Rite in *Textus Roffensis* (Also known as the Cattle-Theft Charm). In Bruce O'Brien and Barbara Bombi, eds., *Textus Roffensis: Law, Language, and Libraries in Early Medieval England*. Turnhout: Brepols: 193–214.

Crick, Julia. (1999) Women, Posthumous Benefaction, and Family Strategy in Pre-Conquest England. *The Journal of British Studies* 38(4): 399–422.

Cubitt, Catherine. (2009) 'As the Lawbook Teaches': Reeves, Lawbooks, and Urban Life in the Anonymous Old English Legend of the Seven Sleepers. *The English Historical Review* 124(510): 1021–49.

(2011) The Politics of Remorse: Penance and Royal Piety in the Reign of Æthelred the Unready. *Historical Research* 85(228): 179–92.

Davies, Anthony. (1989) Witches in Anglo-Saxon England: Five Case Histories. In Donald Scragg, ed., *Superstition and Popular Medicine in Anglo-Saxon England*. Manchester: Manchester Centre for Anglo-Saxon Studies: 41–56.

Fletcher, R.A. (2003) *Bloodfeud: Murder and Revenge in Anglo-Saxon England*. Oxford: Oxford University Press.

Foot, Sarah. (2006) Reading Anglo-Saxon Charters: Memory, Record, or Story? In Elizabeth M. Tyler and Ross Balzaretti, ed., *Narrative and History in the Early Medieval West*. Turnhout: Brepols: 39–67.

Gates, Jay Paul. (2010) *Ealles Englalandes Cyningc*: Cnut's Territorial Kingship and Wulfstan's Paronomastic Play. *The Heroic Age* 14: n.p.

Hollis, Stephanie. (1997) Old English 'Cattle-Theft Charms': Manuscript Contexts and Social Uses. *Anglia* 115(2): 139–64.

Horner, Shari. (2004) The Language of Rape in Old English Literature and Law: Views from the Anglo-Saxon(ist)s. In Carol Braun Pasternack and Lisa M. C. Weston, eds., *Sex and Sexuality in Anglo-Saxon England: Essays in Memory of Daniel Gillmore Calder*. Tempe: Arizona Center for Medieval and Renaissance Studies: 149–83.

Hough, Carole A. (2000) Cattle-Tracking in the Fonthill Letter. *The English Historical Review* 115(463): 864–92.

(2000) Penitential Literature and Secular Law in Anglo-Saxon England. *Anglo-Saxon Studies in Archaeology and History* 11: 133–41.

Hudson, John. (2000) Court Cases and Legal Arguments in England, *c.* 1066–1166. *Transactions of the Royal Historical Society*, 6th series, 10: 91–115.

(2012) *The Oxford History of the Laws of England*, Vol. II: 871–1216. Oxford: Oxford University Press.

Hyams, Paul R. (1981) Trial by Ordeal: The Key to Proof in Early Common Law. In Morris S. Arnold, Thomas A. Green, Sally A. Scully, and Stephen D. White, eds., *On the Laws and Customs of England: Essays in Honor of Samuel E. Thorne*, Chapel Hill: University of North Carolina Press: 90–126.

(1991) The Charter as a Source for the Early Common Law. *The Journal of Legal History* 12(3): 173–89.

(2001) Feud and the State in Late Anglo-Saxon England. *Journal of British Studies* 40(1): 1–43.

(2003) *Rancor and Reconciliation in Medieval England*. Ithaca, NY: Cornell University Press.

(2004) Norms and Legal Argument before 1150. In Andrew Lewis and Michael Lobban, eds. *Law and History*. Oxford: Oxford University Press: 41–61.

Johnson, Tom. (2020) *Law in Common: Legal Cultures in Late-Medieval England*. Oxford: Oxford University Press.

Jurasinski, Stefan. (2015) *The Old English Penitentials and Anglo-Saxon Law*. Cambridge: Cambridge University.

(2019) Royal Law in Wessex and Kent at the Close of the Seventh Century. In Stefan Jurasinski and Andrew Rabin, eds., *Languages of the Law in Early Medieval England: Essays in Memory of Lisi Oliver*. Vol. 22 of Mediaevalia Groningana New Series. Leuven: Peeters: 25–44.

Kamali, Elizabeth Papp. (2019) *Felony and the Guilty Mind in Medieval England*. Cambridge: Cambridge University Press.

Keefer, Sarah Larratt. (1998) *Ut In Omnibus Honorificctur Deus*: The *Corsnæd* Ordeal in Anglo-Saxon England. In John M. Hill and Mary Swan, eds., *The Community, the Family and the Saint: Patterns of Power in Early Medieval Europe*. Turnout: Brepols: 237–64.

(2009) *Ðonne Se Cirlisce Man Ordales Weddieð*: The Anglo-Saxon Lay Ordeal. In Stephen Baxter, Catherine E. Karkov, Janet Nelson and David Pelteret, eds., *Early Medieval Studies in Memory of Patrick Wormald*. Aldershot: Ashgate: 353–68.

Kelly, Susan. (1990) Anglo-Saxon Lay Society and the Written Word. In Rosamond McKitterick, ed., *The Uses of Literacy in Early Medieval Europe*. Cambridge: Cambridge University Press: 36–62

Kennedy, Alan. (1995) Law and Litigation in the *Libellus Æthelwoldi Episcopi*. *Anglo-Saxon England* 24: 131–83.

Keynes, Simon. (1980) *The Diplomas of King Æthelred 'the Unready,' 978–1016*. Cambridge: Cambridge University Press.

(1990) Royal Government and the Written Word in Late Anglo-Saxon England. In Rosamund McKitterick, ed., *The Uses of Literacy in Early Medieval Europe* Cambridge: Cambridge University Press: 226–57.

(1992) The Fonthill Letter. In Michael Korhammer, *Words, Texts, and Manuscripts: Studies in Anglo-Saxon Culture Presented to Helmut Gneuss on the Occasion of His Sixty-Fifth Birthday*. New York: D.S. Brewer: 53–97.

(2007) An Abbot, an Archbishop, and the Viking Raids of 1006–7 and 1009–12. *Anglo-Saxon England* 36: 151–220.

(2005) Wulfsige, Monk of Glastonbury, Abbot of Westminster (c. 990–3), and Bishop of Sherborne (c. 993–1002). In Katherine Barker, David A. Hinton, and Alan Hunt, eds., *St. Wulfsige and Sherborne*. Oxford: Oxbow Books: 53–94.

(2013) Church Councils, Royal Assemblies, and Anglo-Saxon Royal Diplomas. In Gale R. Owen-Crocker and Brian Schneider, eds., *Kingship, Legislation and Power in Anglo-Saxon England*. Woodbridge: Boydell: 17–139.

(2019) The 'Cuckhamsley Chirograph.' In Stefan Jurasinski and Andrew Rabin, eds., *Languages of the Law in Early Medieval England: Essays in Memory of Lisi Oliver*. Vol. 22 of Mediaevalia Groningana New Series. Leuven: Peeters: 193–210.

Lambert, Tom. (2010) "Royal Protections and Private Justice: A Reassessment of Cnut's 'Reserved Pleas.'" In Stefan Jurasinski, Lisi Oliver, and Andrew Rabin, eds., *English Law before Magna Carta: Felix Liebermann and the Gesetze Der Angelsachsen*. Leiden: Brill: 157–76.

(2012) Theft, Homicide and Crime in Late Anglo-Saxon Law. *Past & Present*, 214(1): 3–43.

(2017) *Law and Order in Anglo-Saxon England*. Oxford: Oxford University Press.

Lawson, M. K. (1992) Archbishop Wulfstan and the Homiletic Element in the Laws of Æthelred II and Cnut. *The English Historical Review* 107(424): 565–86.

Marafioti, Nicole. (2019) Crime and Sin in the Laws of Alfred. In Stefan Jurasinski and Andrew Rabin, eds., *Languages of the Law in Early Medieval England: Essays in Memory of Lisi Oliver*. Vol. 22 of Mediaevalia Groningana New Series. Leuven: Peeters: 59–84.

Moilanen, Inka. (2016) The Concept of the Three Orders and Social Mobility in Eleventh-Century England. *The English Historical Review* 131(553): 1331–52.

Musson, Anthony. (2001) *Medieval Law in Context: The Growth of Legal Consciousness from Magna Carta to the Peasants' Revolt*. Manchester: Manchester University Press.

Naismith, Rory. (2011) *Money and Power in Anglo-Saxon England: The Southern English Kingdoms, 757–865*. Cambridge: Cambridge University Press.

Niles, John D. (2009) Trial by Ordeal in Anglo-Saxon England: What's the Problem with Barley? In Stephen Baxter, Catherine E. Karkov, Janet Nelson and David Pelteret, eds., *Early Medieval Studies in Memory of Patrick Wormald*. Aldershot: Ashgate: 369–82.

O'Brien, Bruce. (1996) From Morðor to Murdrum: The Preconquest Origin and Norman Revival of the Murder Fine. *Speculum* 71(2): 321–57.

O'Keeffe, Katherine O'Brien. (1998) Body and Law in Late Anglo-Saxon England. *Anglo-Saxon England* 27: 209–32.

Oliver, Lisi. (2009) Royal and Ecclesiastical Law in Seventh-Century Kent. In Stephen Baxter, Catherine E. Karkov, Janet Nelson, and David Pelteret, eds., *Early Medieval Studies in Memory of Patrick Wormald*. Aldershot: Ashgate: 97–114.

(2011) *The Body Legal in Barbarian Law*. Toronto: University of Toronto Press.

(2015) Genital Mutilation in Germanic Law. In Jay Paul Gates and Nicole Marafioti, eds., *Capital and Corporal Punishment in Anglo-Saxon England*. Woodbridge: Boydell: 48–73.

(2015) Who Wrote Alfred's Laws? In Bruce O'Brien and Barbara Bombi, eds., *Textus Roffensis: Law, Language, and Libraries in Early Medieval England*. Turnhout: Brepols: 231–55.

Pelteret, David. (1995) *Slavery in Early Mediaeval England from the Reign of Alfred until the Twelfth Century*. Woodbridge: Boydell.

Porter, David. (2019) Legal Terminology in the Anglo-Saxon Glossaries. In Stefan Jurasinki and Andrew Rabin, eds., *Languages of the Law: Essays in Memory of Lisi Oliver.* Medievalia Groningana. Leuven: Peeters: 211–24.

Powell, Timothy E. (1994) The 'Three Orders' of Society in Anglo-Saxon England. *Anglo-Saxon England* 23: 103–32.

Putnam, B. H. (1929) "The Transformation of the Keepers of the Peace into the Justices of the Peace 1327–1380." *Transactions of the Royal Historical Society* 12: 19–48.

Rabin, Andrew. (2009) Female Advocacy and Royal Protection in Tenth Century England: The Legal Career of Queen Ælfthryth. *Speculum* 84 (2): 261–88.

(2010) Ritual Magic or Legal Performance? Reconsidering an Old English Charm against Theft. In Stefan Jurasinski, Lisi Oliver, and Andrew Rabin, eds., *English Law before Magna Carta: Felix Liebermann and Die Gesetze Der Angelsachsen.* Leiden: Brill: 177–96.

(2011) Testimony and Authority in Old English Law: Writing the Subject in the 'Fonthill Letter.' In Robert Sturges, ed., *Law and Sovereignty in the Middle Ages and the Renaissance.* Tempe: Arizona Center for Medieval and Renaissance Studies: 147–65.

(2012) Law and Justice. In Jacqueline Stodnick and Renee Trilling, eds., *The Blackwell Handbook of Anglo-Saxon Studies.* Oxford: Blackwell: 85–98.

(2013) Witnessing Kingship: Royal Power and the Legal Subject in the Old English Laws. In Gale R. Owen-Crocker and Brian Schneider, eds., *Kingship, Legislation and Power in Anglo-Saxon England*, Woodbridge: Boydell and Brewer: 219–36.

(2014) Capital Punishment and the Anglo-Saxon Judicial Apparatus: A Maximum View? In Jay Paul Gates and Nicole Marafioti, eds., *Capital and Corporal Punishment in Anglo-Saxon England.* Woodbridge: Boydell: 181–200.

(2015) Courtly Habits: Monastic Women's Legal Literacy in Early Anglo-Saxon England. In Virginia Blanton, Veronica O'Mara and Patricia Stoop, eds., *Nuns' Literacies in Medieval Europe: The Kansas City Dialogue.* Turnhout: Brepols: 179–89.

(2016) Wulfstan at London: Episcopal Politics in the Reign of Æthelred. *English Studies* 97(2): 186–206.

(2018) 'Sharper Than a Serpent's Tooth': Parent–Child Litigation in Anglo-Saxon England. In Susan Irvine and Winfried Rudolph, eds., *Childhood and Adolescence in Anglo-Saxon Literary Culture.* Toronto: University of Toronto Press: 270–90.

Reynolds, Andrew. (2009) *Anglo-Saxon Deviant Burial Practices*. Oxford: Oxford University Press.

Richards, Mary P. (1997) Anglo-Saxonism in the Old English Laws. In Allen J. Frantzen and John D. Niles, eds., *Anglo-Saxonism and the Construction of Social Identity*. Gainesville: University Press of Florida: 40–59.

 (2010) I–II Cnut: Wulfstan's Summa? In Stefan Jurasinski, Lisi Oliver and Andrew Rabin, eds., *English Law before Magna Carta: Felix Liebermann and Die Gesetze Der Angelsachsen*. Leiden: Brill: 137–56.

Rio, Alice. (2017) *Slavery After Rome, 500–1100*. Oxford: Oxford University Press.

Roach, Levi. (2013) *Kingship and Consent in Anglo-Saxon England, 871–978*. Cambridge: Cambridge University Press.

 (2013). Penitential Discourse in the Diplomas of King Æthelred 'the Unready'. *The Journal of Ecclesiastical History* 64(2): 258–76.

Sawyer, P. H. (1968) *Anglo-Saxon Charters: An Annotated List and Bibliography*. London: Royal Historical Society.

Screen, Elina. Anglo-Saxon Law and Numismatics: A Reassessment in the Light of Patrick Wormald's *The Making of English Law*. British Numismatic Society 77: 150–72.

Shoemaker, Karl. (2010) *Sanctuary and Crime in the Middle Ages, 400–1500*. New York: Fordham University Press.

Snook, Ben. (2015) *The Anglo-Saxon Chancery: The History, Language and Production of Anglo-Saxon Charters from Alfred to Edgar*. Woodbridge: Boydell.

 (2015) Who Introduced Charters into England? The Case for Theodore and Hadrian. In Bruce O'Brien and Barbara Bombi, eds., *Textus Roffensis*. Turnhout: Brepols: 257–90.

Thompson, Victoria. (2000) Women, Power, and Protection in Tenth- and Eleventh-Century England. In Noël James Menuge, ed., *Medieval Women and the Law*. Woodbridge: Boydell: 1–17.

Tollerton, Linda. (2011) *Wills and Will-Making in Anglo-Saxon England*. York Medieval Press Series. Woodbridge: Boydell and Brewer.

Whitman, James Q. (2008) *The Origins of Reasonable Doubt: Theological Roots of the Criminal Trial*. New Haven: Yale University Press.

Williams, Ann. (2003) *Æthelred the Unready: The Ill-Counselled King*. London: Hambledon.

Winkler, John Frederick. (1992) Roman Law in Anglo-Saxon England. *Journal of Legal History* 13(2): 101–27.

Wormald, Patrick. (1996) *Iuxta Exempla Romanorum*: The Earliest English Legislation in Context. In Alvar Ellegård and Gunilla Åkerström-Hougen, eds., *Rome and the North*. Jonsered: Åström, 15–27.

(1999) Archbishop Wulfstan and the Holiness of Society. In Patrick Wormald, ed., *Legal Culture in the Early Medieval West: Law as Text, Image, and Experience*. London: Hambledon: 225–52.

(1999) Charters, Law, and the Settlement of Disputes in Anglo-Saxon England. In Patrick Wormald, ed., *Legal Culture in the Early Medieval West: Law as Text, Image, and Experience*. London: Hambledon: 289–312.

(1999) Giving God and King Their Due: Conflict and Its Regulation in the Early English State. In Patrick Wormald, ed., *Legal Culture in the Early Medieval West: Law as Text, Image, and Experience*. London: Hambledon: 333–58.

(1999) A Handlist of Anglo-Saxon Lawsuits. In Patrick Wormald, ed., *Legal Culture in the Early Medieval West: Law as Text, Image, and Experience*. London: Hambledon: 253–88.

(1999) *Lex Scripta* and *Verbum Regis*: Legislation and Germanic Kingship, from Euric to Cnut. In Patrick Wormald, ed., *Legal Culture in the Early Medieval West: Law as Text, Image, and Experience*. London: Hambledon: 1–43.

(1999) Lordship and Justice in the Early English Kingdom: Oswaldslow Revisited. In Patrick Wormald, ed., *Legal Culture in the Early Medieval West: Law as Text, Image, and Experience*. London: Hambledon:313–32.

(1999) *The Making of English Law: King Alfred to the Twelfth Century*. Malden: Blackwell.

(2004) Archbishop Wulfstan: Eleventh-Century Statebuilder. In Matthew Townend ed., *Wulfstan, Archbishop of York: The Proceedings of the Second Alcuin Conference*, Turnhout: Brepols: 9–27.

Acknowledgments

I am deeply grateful to Winfried Rudolf, Emily Thornbury, Rory Naismith, and Megan Cavell, for inviting me to contribute a volume on law to this series. Likewise, many thanks to Elizabeth Friend-Smith of Cambridge University Press for helping smooth the way to publication. Special thanks are due as well to Stefan Jurasinski, Tom Lambert, Kristen Carella, Lindy Brady, Rebecca Brackmann, Nicole Marafioti, Jay Gates, Levi Roach, and the much-missed Lisi Oliver for their conversation, insight, and generosity. The good ideas are theirs, the errors mine.

As always, I want to express my profound gratitude to my wife Shira and my sons Ari and Eli. This book is dedicated to them.

Cambridge Elements ⹀

Elements in England in the Early Medieval World

Megan Cavell
University of Birmingham
Megan Cavell is a Birmingham Fellow in medieval English literature at the University of Birmingham. She works on a wide range of topics in medieval literary studies, from Old and early Middle English and Latin languages and literature to gender, material culture and animal studies. Her previous publications include *Weaving Words and Binding Bodies: The Poetics of Human Experience in Old English Literature* (2016), and she is co-editor of *Riddles at Work in the Anglo-Saxon Tradition: Words, Ideas, Interactions* with Jennifer Neville (forthcoming).

Rory Naismith
University of Cambridge
Rory Naismith is Lecturer in the History of England Before the Norman Conquest in the Department of Anglo-Saxon, Norse and Celtic at the University of Cambridge and a Fellow of Corpus Christi College, Cambridge. Also a Fellow of the Royal Historical Society, he is the author of *Citadel of the Saxons: The Rise of Early London* (2018), *Medieval European Coinage, with a Catalogue of the Coins in the Fitzwilliam Museum, Cambridge, 8: Britain and Ireland c. 400–1066* (2017) and *Money and Power in Anglo-Saxon England: The Southern English Kingdoms 757–865* (2012, which won the 2013 International Society of Anglo-Saxonists First Book Prize).

Winfried Rudolf
University of Göttingen
Winfried Rudolf is Chair of Medieval English Language and Literature in the University of Göttingen (Germany). Recent publications include *Childhood and Adolescence in Anglo-Saxon Literary Culture* with Susan E. Irvine (2018). He has published widely on Anglo-Saxon homiletic literature and is currently principal investigator of the ERC-Project ECHOE– Electronic Corpus of Anonymous Homilies in Old English.

Emily V. Thornbury
Yale University
Emily V. Thornbury is Associate Professor of English at Yale University. She studies the literature and art of early England, with a particular emphasis on English and Latin poetry. Her publications include *Becoming a Poet in Anglo-Saxon England* (2014), and, co-edited with Rebecca Stephenson, *Latinity and Identity in Anglo-Saxon Literature* (2016). She is currently working on a monograph called *The Virtue of Ornament*, about Anglo-Saxon theories of aesthetic value.

About the Series
Elements in England in the Early Medieval World takes an innovative, interdisciplinary view of the culture, history, literature, archaeology and legacy of England between the fifth and eleventh centuries. Individual contributions question and situate key themes, and thereby bring new perspectives to the heritage of Anglo-Saxon England. They draw on texts in Latin and Old English as well as material culture to paint a vivid picture of the period. Relevant not only to students and scholars working in medieval studies, these volumes explore the rich intellectual, methodological and comparative value that the

dynamic researchers interested in the Anglo-Saxon World have to offer in a modern, global context. The series is driven by a commitment to inclusive and critical scholarship, and to the view that Anglo-Saxon studies have a part to play in many fields of academic research, as well as constituting a vibrant and self-contained area of research in its own right.

Cambridge Elements $^{\equiv}$

Elements in England in the Early Medieval World

Elements in the Series

Crime and Punishment in Anglo-Saxon England
Andrew Rabin

A full series listing is available at www.cambridge.org/EASW

CPSIA information can be obtained
at www.ICGtesting.com
Printed in the USA
LVHW040854280721
693861LV00006B/699

9 781108 932035